PUFFIN BOOKS

HAPPY From HEAd to TOE

PUFFIN BOOKS

Puffin Books is part of the Penguin Random House group of companies
whose addresses can be found at global.penguinrandomhouse.com.

www.penguin.co.uk
www.puffin.co.uk
www.ladybird.co.uk

First published 2022

001

Text copyright © Fearne Cotton, 2022
Illustration copyright © Stef Murphy, 2022

The moral right of the author and illustrator has been asserted

Interior design by Sophie Stericker
Printed and bound in Great Britain by Clays Ltd, Elcograf S.p.A.

The authorized representative in the EEA is Penguin Random House Ireland,
Morrison Chambers, 32 Nassau Street, Dublin D02 YH68

A CIP catalogue record for this book is available from the British Library

ISBN: 978–0–241–46671–1

All correspondence to:
Puffin Books, Penguin Random House Children's
One Embassy Gardens, 8 Viaduct Gardens
London SW11 7BW

MIX
Paper from
responsible sources
FSC
www.fsc.org   FSC® C018179

Penguin Random House is committed to a
sustainable future for our business, our readers
and our planet. This book is made from Forest
Stewardship Council® certified paper.

Fearne Cotton

HAPPY From HEAD to TOE

PUFFIN

CONTENTS

INTRODUCTION

Hello! My name is Fearne Cotton.

I'm a presenter and an author, and in my job I get to talk to INCREDIBLE people about mental health and happiness. More importantly, I'm a mum of two kids, Rex and Honey, and step-mum to two teenagers, Arthur and Lola. We spend a lot of time talking about happiness in my family, whether it's when we feel happy and why, or the times when happiness seems to have disappeared. Honey finds happiness when she is drawing, whereas Rex is happiest when he's poking around in rock pools by the sea. Different things bring us joy – there really is no right or wrong when it comes to happiness.

Everyone wants to be happy. But what does happiness feel like to you? For me, it feels as good as eating a giant chocolate cake with thick icing on top and cream in the middle. And if happiness feels this good it makes sense that we want to have it around us whenever we can.

Sometimes we think we can only feel happy if certain things happen – for example, if we get good marks at school, win a game or competition, or get the perfect birthday present. Happiness might show up in those moments, but that type of joy doesn't tend to stick around for long. You may feel good for a few hours – or maybe even all day – but then it begins to fade. This is very normal and is a good reminder that we can't always rely on these moments to feel happy. So what can we do to bring ourselves happiness when it seems to have faded? How can we find our happy whenever we want?

We each have our own happiness supply that lives inside us, but sometimes we all need some help to find it. In this book, I will be suggesting tips for you to feel calmer, confident and happier – even on boring days or during challenging situations.

Happiness is never far away –
we sometimes just need the
right tools to find it.

I want to add a little note here to say that in those times when we don't feel so happy, there is no need to worry. Feeling angry, sad, jealous, annoyed or confused is totally normal and part of being human. We are not meant to feel happy all day every day – that might even get a little bit boring, and take away the magic of the moments when happiness comes and surprises us unexpectedly. Life is constantly changing, and that means we are bound to feel a mixed bag of emotions along the way. So don't worry about happiness disappearing every once in a while – it will come back.

Often, we think happiness just happens in our mind. We believe our brain is running the show and deciding whether we experience happiness or not. But that's not the full story. Think about it for a minute. *Where does our brain live? In a glass jar on a shelf?* No! *On its own little cushion in our room?* Nope! Of course not! It lives in our BODY. Much like our heart or lungs, our brain is a part of our body – we just often talk about it as though it's a separate thing altogether. A happy, healthy mind is so closely connected to a happy, healthy body. How our body feels affects our brain – and this works the other way around too. If we are hungry, haven't slept enough or even if we haven't been able to go for a poo, it'll affect our brain function and our overall happiness. Equally, when our mind feels stressed or overwhelmed, our body reacts. For example, we may experience constipation, headaches or tense muscles in our body or face – it's all connected. When our body is in balance, our mind functions better and vice versa. And, best of all, there are many ways we can look after our bodies to give ourselves a better chance of feeling HAPPY!

I'm going to show you how our remarkable minds and bodies are connected. Give this a try now. Ask a family member or friend to gently massage your shoulder muscles. How does it feel? Hopefully – if they're any good at massaging – you'll feel instantly calmer and maybe even happier. I know this works for me. But if it doesn't work for you try taking one big deep breath in for a count of four:

ONE TWO THREE FOUR

and then gently breathe out for the same amount:

ONE TWO THREE FOUR.

Do this two or three times, and notice how your heartbeat slows down a little and your mind seems to relax, with fewer thoughts and – hopefully – fewer worries racing round it.

In this book we are going to journey through the whole human body to see how we can create even more happiness in our life through that amazing connection between our brain and body. From the top of our head right down to the tips of our toes, there are lots of things that we can do to care for our bodies and make ourselves feel a whole heap better.

Now, as I explained at the start of the book, I'm a presenter and also a writer but I am not an expert on the human body. Everything I have learned has come from trying new things or from being taught by brilliant, clever people who know a lot of cool stuff about how our brains and bodies work. So I've invited them along to give us top tips throughout the book on how to look after our bodies and feel good. Some are doctors, some are great thinkers and some are experts in looking at ways to keep our bodies in balance.

Are you ready to embark on a journey through the human body and discover how to find your happy?

In this book, we'll be going on an adventure through all your extraordinary and clever organs, limbs and body parts. If at any point you get lost and are not sure where in the body we are, come back to this page and take a look!

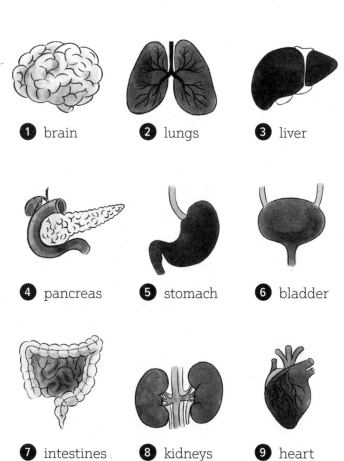

1 brain

2 lungs

3 liver

4 pancreas

5 stomach

6 bladder

7 intestines

8 kidneys

9 heart

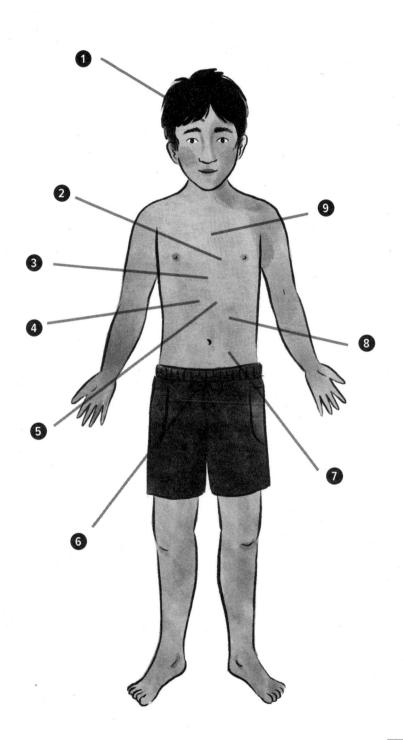

CHAPTER 1

Let's start from the top . . .

HEAD FIRST

We're going to start our journey at the top, and begin by exploring our heads and faces. Each one of us has a head and a face that looks quite different from the next person's. The shape of your head won't be the same as your friend's. The size of your eyes, dip of your nose, colour of your skin, and length and texture of your hair will all differ from those around you. This is just one of the things that makes you uniquely

For example, I have hazel eyes that are quite large, and long blonde hair. I also have a characterful nose that points forward as if it's leading me when I walk.

Now it's your turn! Have a think about what your head looks like.

You could look in the mirror, or you could try tracing your fingers over it to feel the shapes and textures. Does your head feel round or flat at the back? Does your nose feel pointy or curved? Does your skin feel smooth or bumpy? Get to know that wonderful head and face of yours.

No matter what they look like, your head and face are utterly perfect, complex and clever, and, as I said before, totally unique to you.

But even though yours might look different from everyone else's on the planet, each person is able to use their head to feel calmer and happier.

YOUR BRILLIANT BRAIN

Your head contains one of the most precious things – your brain. Your brain is **EXTRAORDINARY**. It controls something called the nervous system, which is the thing that allows your brain to communicate with the rest of your body. The brain allows you to think, move, remember, sleep, dream and feel. But what about the mind? Is that just the same thing as the brain? Not exactly. Your brain is a physical organ in the body whereas your mind isn't. In fact, you can't see it at all. Your mind is the name for the thoughts you have and how you experience and understand the world around you. But here is the really interesting part. Your mind can change your brain. When you are having certain thoughts or experiences, the structure of your brain can change and this is called **NEUROPLASTICITY**.

I love that word. It makes me think of plasticine, which can be moulded into any shape. And you can think of your brain as having that same ability to mould and change based on your experiences. In fact, the brain changes with every new experience you have.

Imagine you had never cleaned your teeth before (gross), then one day you have a new thought – *I'm going to start brushing my teeth every morning and evening from today*. So your mind makes this choice and then your brain and body respond with you brushing your teeth twice a day. From this, the brain starts to rewire based on this new experience so you always remember to clean your teeth each day. A new habit has just been created!

Or, imagine if a large dog barks at you and it makes you nervous (even though you've never been scared of dogs before). Because your mind has experienced fear, that might rewire the brain, which means the next time you see a dog you might feel scared again. Luckily, though, that can change. And this chapter is going to be about how you can use your mind to change how your brain is structured. This will help you create new habits and reactions – and hopefully help you feel happier and less worried!

I should tell you now: I am not a brain doctor, nor a scientist. I'm just someone who has a huge interest in the human brain and happiness, and handily I also have a brain myself!

But, as powerful and fascinating as your brilliant brain is, the story of happiness doesn't just start and end there . . .

Over the last few years, one of the biggest discoveries I've made when speaking to people about what makes them happy is that most of us believe all our happiness comes from our brain. But the brain is not the only driving force behind how we feel, and if it WAS, this book would be called *Happy from Head to* . . . err *Head*! (It would also be rather short.) The truth is,

HAPPINESS IS A FULL-BODY EXPERIENCE.

So while we will explore our clever brains in this chapter, they are only the tip of the iceberg!

It's time to meet our first expert: my friend **Kimberley Wilson**. Kimberley is a psychologist and nutritionist, which means she studies the brain, emotions and human behaviour, and how food affects people's health. Kimberley helps people understand how their brains and bodies react to the world around them and to the food they eat. She is going to tell us a bit more about the mind-boggling brain before we get started. Because if we are going to understand how our brains can bring us joy, we first have to understand a little more about how this mysterious part of our body works.

Kimberley Wilson, psychologist and nutritionist

So, Kimberley, tell us: what exactly are thoughts?
Thoughts are the activities in your brain that you
are aware of. Your brain is constantly doing stuff: for
example, it monitors your body temperature to make
sure you don't get too hot or too cold, and it also tells
you when you're thirsty and hungry. But these and
many other activities happen without you realizing.
You don't have to try; they just happen. We call these
activities 'unconscious'. But if you are telling a friend
about what you did yesterday, or trying to remember
someone's name or imagining something you will
do in the future, you are aware that your brain is
working on something.

This is thinking.

What is happening in the brain when we have a thought?

Your brain is made up of lots of brain cells that are connected – just like the way different areas in a city are connected by streets. In a city, you might have an area where most of the schools are. There might be another where all the shops are. And maybe another area with a playground. There will be different patterns of activity in and around these areas – for example, at the end of the school day, some students will go to the playground and some will go to the shops. So there is a pattern of activity between the school, the playground and the shops as they become busier.

And the same thing happens in your brain! Your experiences of life and all the things you know are arranged in millions of connected areas in your brain.

And when you are thinking, it means the different areas in your brain are interacting.

Do all brains work in the same way?
All brains work slightly differently. Some people think in words, and some in pictures. Some people are more laid-back, while others are more alert. The way your brain is built will depend on many things, like how your family's brains are built, the food you eat and much more. Your brain is also influenced by the experiences you have in life.

Since we all have different experiences, no one's brain works in the exact same way as somebody else's.

What happens in the brain and body when we are happy?
Different things will make us happy at certain times. Sometimes we are happy lying in bed. Sometimes we are happy being active. We might be one type of happy with our family and another with our friends.

Your body and brain produce a range of chemicals that are linked to feelings of happiness. One chemical is called **dopamine**, and it's released when we are looking forward to something. Another chemical, called **oxytocin**, is released when we are with people we care about. Other chemicals called **endorphins** are released when we eat food we like. When we are happy, our body makes these chemicals that help us feel relaxed and safe.

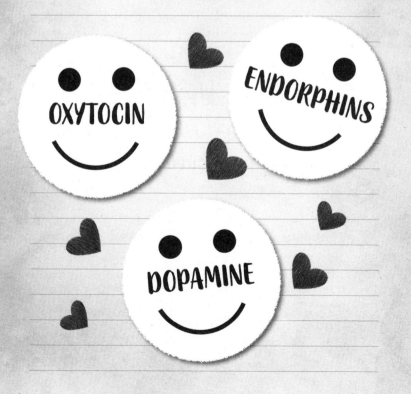

Why does our body react when we have certain thoughts? For example, why do our muscles tense when we are nervous, and why does our heart rate slow down when we think calming thoughts?

Your brain is always trying to predict what you will need to do next and how much energy it will take. And it does this without us even realizing! To make these predictions, it uses information about things that have happened in the past as well as information about where you are and what you are doing at any given moment. The important thing to remember is that your brain can't really tell the difference between when you are actually doing something or when you are just thinking about it.

Here's an example: when you line up at the start of a race, you might feel your breathing and your heart rate speeding up. This is because your brain is predicting that you will need more oxygen pumping through your body to power your muscles as you run. Even if you just lie in bed the night before and think about the race, your heart rate might still speed up because your brain doesn't know that you are just imagining it. Your brain treats your thoughts – whether they are past memories or future worries – as if they are happening right now.

If you find yourself in a situation that you have never been in before or that you are unsure about, your brain can't predict what you will need to do, so it will just assume that you will need lots of energy to deal with it.

To give you a quick burst of energy, your body releases a chemical called **cortisol**, and one of the side effects of cortisol is that it can give you butterflies in your tummy. Basically, the sensations that you experience when you are nervous, frightened or worried are side effects of your brain preparing your body for action.

Are there ways in which we can train our brains to think more positively?

Being more positive or confident is mostly about practice. For example, if you had to get up on stage and sing in front of 1,000 people for the first time, you would probably feel quite nervous. So to prepare, it would be a good idea to start small.

1. Practise singing by yourself
2. Try in front of one person
3. Sing in front of five people

Each time you practise, you give your brain more information that will help it predict what will happen. Then when you do perform for 1,000 people, there is more chance that it will be a great success!

A CONFIDENT OR
POSITIVE PERSON IS
JUST SOMEONE
WHOSE BRAIN IS MORE
USED TO MAKING
PREDICTIONS
OF SUCCESS - AND
THAT COMES WITH
PRACTICE.

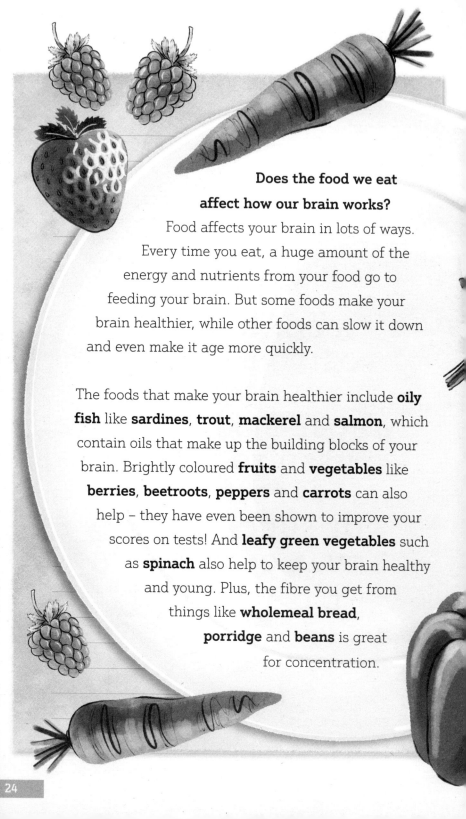

Does the food we eat affect how our brain works?

Food affects your brain in lots of ways. Every time you eat, a huge amount of the energy and nutrients from your food go to feeding your brain. But some foods make your brain healthier, while other foods can slow it down and even make it age more quickly.

The foods that make your brain healthier include **oily fish** like **sardines**, **trout**, **mackerel** and **salmon**, which contain oils that make up the building blocks of your brain. Brightly coloured **fruits** and **vegetables** like **berries**, **beetroots**, **peppers** and **carrots** can also help – they have even been shown to improve your scores on tests! And **leafy green vegetables** such as **spinach** also help to keep your brain healthy and young. Plus, the fibre you get from things like **wholemeal bread**, **porridge** and **beans** is great for concentration.

Unfortunately, eating too much sugar in the form of sweets, chocolates and sweetened drinks can hurt your brain. While small amounts of sugar are fine (and tasty), lots of sugar can negatively affect the parts of your brain that organize memories, possibly making it harder to learn. It can also lower the levels of an important chemical in your brain that helps it to grow.

IMAGINE THIS ...

One of the coolest things about the brain is that we can use it to imagine. Daydreaming and coming up with ideas are some of my favourite hobbies. When I was at school, I would spend a lot of time staring out of the window, dreaming of fantasy situations that made me feel happy. I found maths lessons really difficult and using my brain to work out sums felt almost impossible – yet I could easily conjure up images of myself on stage, dancing and prancing with an audience in front of me, cheering!

WHAT DO YOU LIKE TO DAYDREAM ABOUT?

While I'm not necessarily telling you to spend your time in the classroom coming up with imaginary situations, there are lots of good things that can come from finding some time alone with your mind to daydream. Daydreaming can help us to create little slices of happiness in our day. In fact, it can sometimes change our entire mood altogether ...

DAYDREAMER

Remember how Kimberley said that your heart rate can speed up when you think about a race, even if you're actually lying in bed? Let's try this out ourselves!

Imagine that you are on the starting line of a race track. You look ahead at the looming dark-red track, and down at your feet in your sparkling white trainers, nervously fidgeting away. There is a huge crowd lining the athletics stadium – hands are in the air waving banners with your name on, and there are shouts of encouragement, and camera flashes going off. You have runners either side of you, all looking very focused and ready to race against you. If you really use your imagination to put yourself in that position, can you feel a little rush around your body? Is your heart racing a little faster than before? It's incredible that our body can react to a situation that is only happening in our imagination. Yet it feels so real!

Now...

Try thinking of a place that makes you happy. Is it in a woodland among tall pine trees? By a stream that is sparkling in the sunlight? There are no rules, it can literally be anywhere that makes you feel good.

Take your time so you really picture yourself there. Has your heart rate slowed down? Have the corners of your mouth smiled peacefully? Does your body feel more at ease? Do you see how your imagination can help you to feel good and more relaxed?

This means that you can use your imagination to bring you calmness and joy in the moments when you need it most. For example, if there is a time when you feel very nervous about having to speak in public, you can try to use your imagination to picture a peaceful or happy scene. This should help calm your body and mind before you start. You might find that it brings a little slice of happiness into your day.

If you aren't sure where your happy place is yet – that's OK! I'm going to show you mine, and maybe this will work for you too.

Picture a beautiful beach. The sand is soft and pale, and the sea is calm and turquoise as it laps at the shore. There is a comfy sun lounger with a towel laid out on it, and your name is stitched into the fabric.

You lie down and stretch your legs and arms out, feeling the warmth of the sun hitting your body.

Do you feel calm and relaxed?

DON'T BE SCARED

Our imagination can help us dream our way into situations, and it can also help us to write stories, come up with ideas and solve problems. At other times, our imagination can run away with itself, leaving us feeling a little out of control. Have you ever felt scared or worried before you go to bed? Sometimes at night, once the light goes out, our imagination can take over – whether that's thinking about things from the day that have made you upset or anxious, or even fear of being in a dark room. When your mind is filled with worries, it's hard to feel calm and happy – and **IMPOSSIBLE** to get to sleep!

When we think about things that make us anxious, our body will react with fear. For example, suppose you see a scary image of a shark on the television one day. Then, just as you get into bed, you start to imagine the shark swimming up the pipes into your bathroom and then chasing you into your bedroom. In this situation, your brain is probably creating images of a **TERRIFYING** shark with large vicious teeth and beady eyes.

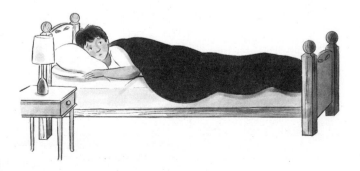

Whatever it is that makes you anxious – whether it's sharks or spiders or darkness or anything else – you are likely to find that your heart beats faster when you think about it. Your breathing might also be quicker than normal. Your imagination is telling you that you're in danger, so your body thinks you *are* in danger.

As tricky as it might feel, next time this happens, why not try to focus on positive stories and images? You can train your imagination to change the story so it has a different ending. Perhaps the shark swims into your room and, all of a sudden as it comes into view, you notice that it is wearing big magnifying goggles that make its eyes look **HILARIOUS**. And it has long rabbit teeth that extend below its jawline, or a funny cartoon voice that **BOOMS** across the room and makes you laugh. It might even burst into song and start dancing around with its fins flapping. Then it says goodnight to you before swimming off to find its friends. With this new story in your mind, hopefully you will find yourself smiling and laughing, and your body will calm down and feel ready for a restful night of sleep.

Remember, you always have the power to change the storyline of your daydreams – even before bed.

NIGHTMARES

Did you know that sometimes your brain is more active when you're asleep than when you're awake? If you tend to have dreams at night, then maybe you knew this already. A nightmare is a bad dream. Most people get them once in a while, no matter how old they are. They can make us feel nervous, worried or sad. The best thing to remember is that nightmares are very common and – most important of all –

THEY ARE NOT REAL.

One way to find comfort might be to speak to either your parent or the grown-up you live with or a sibling if you wake up in the night. But while you are having nightmares, it's a little trickier to train your brain to think happy thoughts, as you are asleep and have less control over your own mind in that moment. What you can do is try to remember these helpful things before you go to sleep and after you wake up:

Think of your mind like a filing cabinet, containing all the information from your life and experiences in separate folders.

When you go to sleep, your brain takes all the information from that day and files away your thoughts into these folders.

A nightmare is usually just your wonderful, complicated brain trying to sort through these files and make sense of all you have seen, heard and experienced recently.

Nothing you're seeing is actually happening at that moment, so it can't harm you.

In the morning you may feel a little more tired and still worried about your nightmare, but that's because your brain was working hard throughout the night putting together lots of your recent feelings and experiences into a story.

Our imagination is an incredible tool once we understand how it works. The best and most powerful thing we can do is realize that we have more control over it than we might have first thought. This allows us to turn those moments when we're feeling sad, nervous or anxious into moments when we might just feel a bit happier and more relaxed – even when we're sleeping!

Someone I know who uses their imagination to help them feel great and achieve extraordinary things is Olympic diver and gold medallist, **Tom Daley**.

Tom started diving when he was seven years old and took part in his first Olympic Games aged fourteen. Diving in such big global competitions means that Tom has to deal with a lot of pressure. Picture it now: you're standing at the top of an incredibly high diving board, with a large crowd of people sitting below in the stands, the other divers watching nearby too, and – oh – also

MILLIONS

of people watching you live on the TV.

Sounds nerve-racking, right?

Tom uses his imagination to help him feel calmer and perform well in competitions. He practises something called visualization, which is when you imagine a certain outcome of the thing you're about to do. Tom is going to give us some tips for how to cope with moments of stress, pressure and nerves, and find calmness and joy.

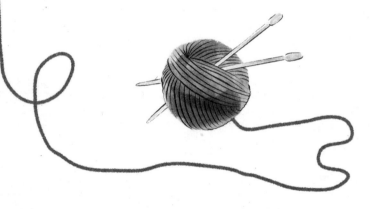

He's also going to tell us about a technique he uses called mindfulness to prepare for a big event like the Olympics. Mindfulness means putting all your focus and attention into something. You can be mindful with any activity as long as you're taking your time and noticing what you're doing. This can help to relax your mind and body. For Tom, his activity of choice is knitting. He finds it very calming, particularly when he is waiting around in between dives, as his brain can only focus on that one task at hand. All other worries, problems and fears have to move over in that moment when you're focusing on the mindful activity.

Tom Daley, Olympic diver

Tom, the pressure of diving in a competition like the Olympics must be massive. How do you use visualization for a big dive when the pressure is on?

Visualization comes in lots of different forms. I do two versions of it before every single dive. First, when I'm halfway up the diving board, I imagine that I'm watching myself on TV doing the perfect dive. I don't think about anything except the best version of the dive. This is really difficult sometimes – especially when I first started trying to do visualization – because things would creep into my mind and I'd end up visualizing the dive going wrong.

But practice makes perfect with skills in the real world, and it's the same with skills in your head, so you have to keep trying.

The second version of visualization I do is when I go up to the next level of the platform. Here, I pretend to be in the dive already, and I imagine exactly what I'm going to see, hear, smell and feel as I'm spinning round. This helps prepare me for the big moment and makes me much calmer before I start.

What do you do if you find your mind wandering?
That's something that happens often. As soon as anything goes wrong in my visualized dive, I start again and do not allow myself to go all the way through to the end until it's right. As soon as things start to go a little bit wrong, I stop and start again. It's something that I've practised over and over again. Like anything – whether it's the first time you try and tie your shoelaces or the first time you try and ride a bike – chances are that it's not going to work the first time, so you try again, and again, and again. I think lots of people forget that exercising your brain is just as important as exercising your body.

> Your brain is a muscle and you have to work it like you would work anything else to make it stronger.

How do knitting and crochet help clear your mind?
They were my secret weapons during the run-up to the 2020 Olympics because there was so much time to overthink during lockdown, when we weren't allowed to go out; we weren't allowed to see friends; we weren't allowed to do so many things that we'd normally be able to do. So to have that little escape, when I'd have to just focus on every stitch that was in front of me, and I couldn't be distracted or be thinking about other things was a great mindfulness activity. Knitting and crocheting allowed me to be really present and creative outside of diving.

What are the benefits of mindfulness?

I brushed mindfulness off at the beginning. I thought:

this isn't for me

this is not going to work

it's annoying

it takes up so much time ...

But when I allowed myself to truly focus on practising mindfulness for just ten minutes every day, it really started to make a difference. I found after a few weeks it allowed me to feel a lot calmer, and less anxious and more confident when I was diving. It also allowed me to perform better in competitions, because I had coping mechanisms for when I felt nervous.

Tom recently sent me some knitting needles and a few balls of brightly coloured wool in the post, so I'm going to give it a try. I might knit a scarf or a hat, or maybe I could knit a little jumper for my cat, Keloy. Now that would be cute!

While I might not be willing to throw myself off a really tall diving board anytime soon, I know that trying knitting could help me feel calmer and happier just like it did for Tom. Perhaps you could give it a try as well!

A HOLIDAY FOR THE BRAIN

Our brain works really hard all day and night, so it's no surprise that it needs a little holiday every now and then. When we don't give our brain time to switch off, we can become irritable or start to worry about things more than we need to.

Can you think of any hobbies or activities that give your brain a little moment to rest? Perhaps when you're out on a bike ride or doing something creative like writing or drawing?

I love watching TV, as it helps me to switch off from thinking about my own life and focus on something else – and there is nothing wrong with that. But we do need to think about how long we end up sitting in front of the screen for. If you do it for too long it can sometimes have the opposite effect and prevent you from relaxing at all! When we watch television, we are still taking in a lot of information. Your brain might be remembering all the characters' names in a movie, or getting excited or nervous watching a tense scene. Your brain is still having to do a lot of work – even though you feel like you're resting – so limiting your time in front of the TV and finding other activities to do instead is a good idea.

SOMETIMES, THE **BEST THING** FOR A TIRED BRAIN IS A BIT OF **FUN!**

Here are some peaceful activities you could do to really help your brain switch off and get the rest it truly deserves. Some of these allow you to get creative and express yourself, while others just give you a chance to release some energy. Either way, the best thing to do is find one that helps you relax, smile and enjoy yourself!

1. Drawing
2. Making a scrapbook
3. Writing a poem or song
4. Flying a kite
5. Swimming
6. Baking cakes
7. Modelling clay
8. Origami
9. Creating your own cartoon strip
10. Going on a walk with a relative or friend

Personally, I love to go on long walks with my family. Sometimes I will spend time looking around at the different trees or watching out for interesting wildlife. Maybe your peaceful hobby is different from mine, your friends' or your family's, and that's OK. It doesn't matter what it is or for how long you do it; it's just a lovely way to give your brain a little holiday every now and then.

Some people like to just sit quietly and notice the thoughts that are coming into their head. This is called meditating, and it's a very effective way of giving your brain a rest. There are different ways you can do it: some people sit and do nothing, some listen to music, some go for a walk, some listen to something called a guided meditation, which is when somebody talks you through how to relax.

My friend **Adam Martin** is a meditation teacher. He is here to explain why meditation is so great and has some top tips for how to try it yourself.

Adam Martin, meditation teacher

How would you describe meditation?

Meditation has been practised in cultures all over the world for many years. It is the act of reflecting and taking charge of your mind. Some people think the point is for you to have no thoughts at all but that is actually impossible. You can meditate in lots of different ways, such as by focusing, relaxing or thinking. It involves noticing the thoughts you are having, and watching each thought pass by like clouds in the sky. You can do it by sitting with your eyes closed peacefully and just listening to your own breathing, but if that feels too tricky you could walk or even dance. Practising a mindful activity is also a form of meditation.

What is a guided meditation?

A guided meditation is when a teacher is helping you focus your mind. It's like the difference between letting your imagination run wild or reading a book. So, you can either sit still and close your eyes and see what pops into your head, or you could listen to somebody guide you towards thinking calming thoughts.

How does meditation make you feel?

Meditation makes me feel that this moment right now is magical. I am not thinking about the past or the future, but simply being in the present and enjoying it for what it is.

How does meditation help you to feel calmer and happier?

Life can sometimes feel overwhelming. Meditation helps to balance your brain and bring quiet to the busyness of life. In scientific terms, meditation activates something called your **GABA neurotransmitter**, which is the part of the brain that helps you feel calm and content.

What should you do if you find it hard to sit still?

Why not try this? Find a tree you like the look of then place your hands on it. Close your eyes and at first just focus on your breath. Don't change a thing, just focus as you breathe in and out. Listen as your breath begins to gently calm. Now switch your awareness to the tree. Notice what the bark of the tree feels like and its temperature. You could even repeat a sentence like this: 'I am exactly where I need to be', or any other positive phrase that makes you feel good and calm and allows you to enjoy the present moment.

Is there a good time of day to meditate?

In the morning, our brain has not yet fully woken up and so it can be a little easier to focus. But rather than thinking about meditating at just one specific time of day, try and think about lots of little times – perhaps a minute here or five minutes there. You can make meditation something that you practise throughout the day.

How often should I meditate?

There's no correct answer to this question – you should do it whenever you can and whenever it feels right! For example, if you feel overwhelmed or anxious, make the time to focus your mind, listen to your breathing and let your thoughts come and go.

FEELING GREEN

Happiness is wonderful – that's why I've written lots of books about it, and even have a podcast called 'Happy Place'! But I don't want to give all the other emotions a bad name, because they are all super normal. Nobody feels happy all the time. There are so many things that can happen in life that affect how we feel, and there's no such thing as bad emotions. Some don't feel as great as happiness and are harder to deal with, but they're common and there's nothing wrong with you feeling these other types of emotions. In fact, we can learn a lot from them. Usually, they are trying to tell us something important.

Have you ever felt jealous before? Maybe of a friend who got a better mark in a test, or a sibling who seems to be better at something than you, like sport or singing or dancing? While jealousy doesn't feel good, remember that it is there to try to tell you something. For example, maybe it's trying to tell you that you would feel better if you got a higher mark, and you should spend some more time studying that subject. Or maybe it's telling you that you need to find your own hobby that you're great at, rather than comparing yourself to your sibling. See how jealousy can actually be quite handy? It's the same with most emotions. There is always something to learn from them.

SOMEONE ELSE'S WORDS

Sometimes you can feel stuck in an emotion that you don't enjoy. While you can try and work out what this emotion is trying to tell you, you can also remind yourself these three important words: it will pass. No emotion sticks around forever.

BUT SOMETIMES OUR BRAINS GRAB HOLD OF NEGATIVE INFORMATION AND THEN GET STUCK, MAKING IT HARD TO MOVE ON FROM CERTAIN FEELINGS.

For example, if a person says something mean to you, it can feel very tricky to ignore what they've said. Sometimes our brains will take that comment and start to believe it's true. Our brain forgets that it wasn't our idea in the first place.

Let me explain. I used to go to ballet classes, which I loved.
Each week I would look forward to putting on my leotard and
dancing about in my satin shoes. Every now and then we would
have to take an exam. Things worked a bit differently on exam
days – we had to wear our best, smartest leotard, and have
our hair neatly pulled back into a tight, shiny bun. In the
changing room, me and a few other kids waited nervously
for our names to be called. One other girl looked over at my
neatly slicked-back hair and said,

> # You have a big forehead – you look a bit like an
> # EGG!

Now, I had never had this thought before. I rarely wore my hair
like this and hadn't noticed the size of my forehead. But all
of a sudden I imagined my head as a giant egg, sitting on top
of my neck and gleaming in the harsh changing-room lights.
I felt embarrassed and like there might be something wrong
with me. I still to this day don't like to wear my hair pulled back

because of that one comment. And that was thirty years ago! Can you see how my brain took someone else's words and started to believe they were true? Another person's opinion changed my own way of thinking.

With practice we can change this, and train our brain to not automatically believe everything it hears. The smartest thing to do is to question the comments that come your way and not just accept them. If someone says something unkind, just ask yourself:

Is that true?
Do I really believe that?

Because what you believe about yourself is so much more important than what someone else believes. It might still make you feel sad or angry when someone says something hurtful, but maybe – just maybe – by questioning those comments you'll remember that you are a wonderful, smart, brilliant, bright and unique human – no matter what anyone else says. Just keep saying out loud, or in your head, or in front of a mirror:

I AM AMAZING!

(Because it's true!)

TOP TIPS
FOR A HAPPY HEAD:

Remember which foods will help your brain's health, such as colourful fruit and veg.

If you have a negative thought or hear a mean comment, question it!

Practise visualization.

Turn scary thoughts into funny images – like a shark wearing goggles, a spider on a skateboard or a monster under the bed doing karaoke!

Try meditating or find an activity where you can practise mindfulness.

Find a hobby or activity that allows your brain to take a well-deserved holiday.

Find a happy place and use your imagination to picture it when you're feeling stressed.

Remember that you are AMAZING!

CHAPTER 2

Your fantastic face

LET'S FACE IT...

First up, may I say you have the MOST BRILLIANT face.

IT'S SO...

YOU!

You can show so many emotions with your face. When you scrunch up your nose, it is clear that you do not like the food in front of you. When you grin and your teeth are on show, it's obvious how happy you are. And when your eyes are as big as dinner plates, everyone knows you are surprised.

Did you know the colossal squids' eyes are ACTUALLY as big as dinner plates ALL THE TIME? I wonder how they let others know when they're surprised . . .

When you meet new people, your
face is the first thing they see. Your
brilliant face has so much going on, and
there are many ways that we can use
its different features to find happiness.

LOOK INTO MY EYES

It is through our eyes that we see the world and they can bring us so much joy – depending on what we use them for.

Look for something in the room you're in now that makes you smile. It could be a photo that you love, or a cute pet (if you have one), or maybe you're wearing your favourite piece of clothing. As I write this, I'm looking at a bunch of flowers on my desk that my next-door neighbour gave to me. The flowers are orange, red and purple and make me smile when I look at them. Do you feel a little happier when you look at your chosen object?

NOTICING THINGS THAT CHEER US UP IS IMPORTANT WHEN IT COMES TO HAPPINESS.

If we are only focused on seeing stuff that makes us unhappy, we are likely to see even more things that make us unhappy.

For example, let's say you were excited to go outside, but then it starts raining so you have to stay in. You're likely to feel in a bad mood, and so your mind might focus on the negatives rather than the positives of being unexpectedly stuck indoors. You might feel bored and exclaim that there is nothing to do, or start to find your family PARTICULARLY annoying to be around that day. In these moments, by focusing on the negatives, it can feel as though you're surrounded by things that make you unhappy.

BUT what if you turned the situation on its head by choosing to use your eyes and your mind to find some of the positives? OK, so you can't go outside like you wanted to, but take a look around. Could you search the house and see if there's anything lying around for you to get crafty and creative with? Is there a bag of flour and some eggs that you could whip up into a delicious cake that you could then eat? Or can you spot a book on your bedside table that you've wanted to read for a while but haven't found the time – could you finally start it? The day doesn't look so bad now, does it? Sometimes we need to remind ourselves that we can **choose to see the positives.** When we do that, we allow ourselves to feel happy even when things are getting us down.

Your eyes have an extraordinary ability to absorb tons of things that bring you joy! And you can choose what you use them for. So read books that make you feel great, observe the wonders of nature that are all around you, and when you are having some screen time choose positive television shows to watch that revolve around wonderful, kind characters or wildlife.

As I mentioned, I love to walk. If I am feeling stressed or sad about something, I pop into the local park and let my eyes linger on the colours of the leaves and the different tones in the sky. This morning the sky was orange and pink and looked fiery. Focusing on its beauty made me happy and grateful to be out in nature.

AN ATTITUDE OF GRATITUDE!

Sometimes when you're feeling low, it's hard to remember the things around you that do bring you joy. If school is making you feel stressed, or you've fallen out with someone, it's not always as simple as using your eyes to focus on things that make you happy. One thing I've discovered that's really helpful is making a list of things that I'm grateful for – and the best time to do this is on a day when I'm in a good mood. This way, when I'm next in a bad mood, I can look back on my list and remind myself of the things that make me smile. Here's my list from today:

I'm grateful for:

1. Having the time to get creative and paint pictures.
2. My peaceful cat.
3. A funny chat I had with a friend.
4. I did some exercise, which made me feel good.
5. The colourful sky.

Now it's your turn! Can you list five positive things about yourself, your life or the world around you that you are thankful for?

Now look at that list of happy, brilliant things. When we focus on the positives, we have less time to focus on the negatives. Next time you're feeling down and struggling to see the sunny side, pick up this list. It might just remind you of all the things that you love about your life, and hopefully help you find joy that day!

RAINBOW POWER

Different colours can make us feel certain emotions. What is the first colour that springs to mind when you think about anger? For me, it's red. If I ask you to think of sadness, what colour springs to mind? What about calmness?

Now, what is your happy colour?

Once you have discovered your happy colour, can you think of some ways to bring it into your life more? I have a friend called Sophie Robinson who is an expert in colour and how to add it to your home. Sophie has a brightly coloured home that makes you feel like you're walking through a rainbow. Her walls are dark blue, her doors are sunshine yellow and her furniture has splashes of every other colour you can think of. She once gave me a great idea when

Rex's bedroom needed a lick of paint. Sophie advised me to give Rex a colour chart to pick his happy colour, and he quickly pointed to a vibrant aquamarine that reminded him of the ocean – his favourite subject! We chose this colour for his walls and it has given Rex's bedroom an underwater feel, which is very peaceful and relaxing at night-time.

Even if you aren't able to completely redecorate your room, can you think of objects in your happy colour that you could put in there? Then, every time you go to your room, you will see that colour and hopefully it will make you smile. You could even wear more of that colour so you are quite literally walking around with happiness.

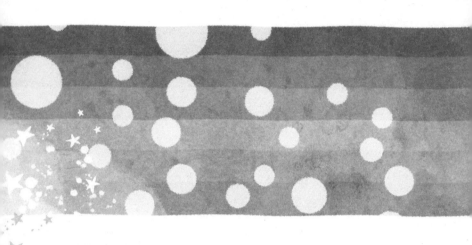

YOUR OTHER SENSES

Do you wear glasses or contact lenses to help you see?
For many people, this can improve their eyesight. But
some people who have impaired vision or are blind can
either see very little or cannot see anything at all. There
are around 40 million people in the world who are blind,
and another 250 million who have some form of visual
impairment. Some people are born without sight, and some
may have an illness or accident that causes them to lose it.

Betsy Griffin is a brilliant eight-year-old girl who talks on
her YouTube channel – Betsy's Positive Videos – about her
experience of being blind. When Betsy was very young, she
had something called a brain tumour, which affected her
eyesight. A brain tumour is the name for a lump in the brain
that doesn't belong there, and in Betsy's case doctors were

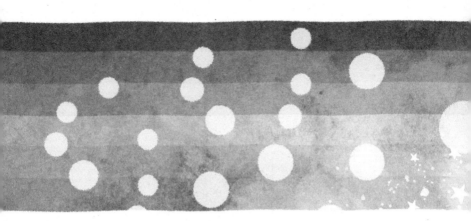

able to remove a part of the lump with an operation, and give her medicine to stop the tumour from growing further. Betsy's mission is to bring positivity to the world with her sunny attitude and wise thoughts. I love watching Betsy's videos and have learned a lot from her – you should watch some too if you can!

Because Betsy can't see the world around her clearly, she uses her other senses to move around. She also reads Braille – a form of written language that is made up of patterns of raised dots which represent letters of the alphabet or whole words. To read, Betsy runs her fingers over the page and feels the little bumps on it with her fingertips. She also reads 'feely' books that have raised pictures so she can visualize what she's reading about too. Let's find out more about how Betsy uses her other senses.

Hi Betsy, how are you today?

I am **spandandall**, thank you. That's a word I've made up by mixing all these good words together: happy, excited, joyful, smiley, jolly, fantastic.

I think I'm going to start using that word! Can you tell me about how you use Braille?

Braille is lots of raised dots – also known as cells – that make up different letters. Sometimes one cell can be a couple of letters or even a whole word. I use Braille for reading and writing. I have a Perkins Brailler, which is like a typewriter but for Braille. I also have a Braillenote, which is like a computer. My fingers are really sensitive, which helps me read

Braille. My mum's fingers aren't quite as sensitive so when she feels the Braille, the dots all feel the same – but I can tell the difference.

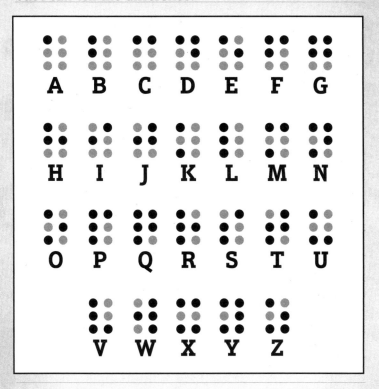

How long did it take you to learn how to read Braille?

Maybe four or five years. I started in nursery and I am still learning stuff now. I did a lot of work on growing my finger sensitivity before learning how to read

Braille. It was all quite fun. I'm now really good at reading – one of the best in my class at school.

When you are feeling the paper and touching the dots on the page, are you imagining the story and images in your mind?

I picture everything: the smells, the feel, the look of it all. At the moment I'm reading *Ratburger* by David Walliams, so I'm picturing the prawn cocktail crisps that are described in the book and that smell wafting down the corridor. Even though I don't like prawn cocktail crisps one bit! I love when stories are described in such detail that all the senses are brought to life.

How do you use your other senses in your everyday life to bring you joy?

I use all my senses, whether I'm doing my school work or at a party. My hearing is very important as I love listening to music. My taste has become heightened too as I really appreciate my food. I love fish pie, shepherd's pie – all the pies. My favourite fruit is watermelon; I love the texture and the taste and how juicy it is.

I know you have cuddly toys. Which is your favourite at the moment and what does it feel like to touch?

My tiger is sooo big and soft and he keeps me very comfortable. I always love very soft toys and I love my clothes being really soft too. Touch is very important to me. I even like the texture of slime!

I loved hearing what Betsy had to say about her senses, and how her sense of touch and hearing are heightened because she can't use her sense of sight. But, as Betsy explains, even without her vision her other senses can be just as effective in bringing her joy! If you are interested to know what Braille or a Braillenote computer look like, there are lots of photos online that you can have a look at.

WHO NOSE?

What is your favourite smell? Mine is cakes baking in the oven, and Rex's and Honey's faces! I'm constantly trying to sniff my children as they smell so lovely, even if it slightly annoys them. So how can we use this sense to bring joy to our day?

Remember when we discovered that our imagination can change things within our body, like the speed of our heartbeat and our breathing? Smell can do the same thing. When we smell something we like, it can make us feel a certain emotion. Have you ever gone to a swimming pool and found the smell of chlorine makes you feel happy? This might be because as the smell reaches your nose, it sends a signal to your brain, which brings up lovely memories of summer holidays. Or maybe there is another smell that makes you feel good and brings back wonderful memories.

Just like you did with your happy colour, think about your happy smells. Then, see if there are ways to bring those smells into your life more. If it's the smell of freshly cut grass, go visit the park! If it's the smell of baking, you could bake something with a family member at the weekend. These little actions can bring you snippets of joy in such an easy way.

If you feel scared at night-time, there are certain smells that might help you feel a little calmer and happier. If Honey is feeling worried, I sometimes spritz lavender spray by her bed before she goes to sleep. Lavender is known to be a very calming smell. And now her nose and brain work as a team to remind her that every time she smells lavender her body can relax.

YOUR SENSE OF
SMELL AND YOUR
CLEVER NOSE CAN
HELP BRING BACK
HAPPY MEMORIES
AND MAKE YOU
FEEL CALMER
WHENEVER
YOU NEED IT.

YOUR MAGICAL MOUTH

Go and have a look in the mirror now and make the biggest, toothiest grin you can.

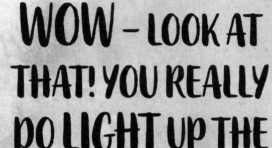

WOW – LOOK AT THAT! YOU REALLY DO **LIGHT** UP THE ROOM WITH THAT **BRILLIANT** SMILE OF YOURS.

When you smile do you feel happier? What other shapes can you make with your mouth? Try yawning, then grimacing, and maybe even blowing a kiss. Your mouth is one of the most expressive parts of your face and body, and it lets the world know if you are feeling happy, excited, sad and more.

But that's not all the mouth does – it's a very busy part of our face! We use it every day to breathe. And to eat. And to talk. And to laugh. It's easy to take our mouth for granted and forget how much it does for us each day.

A PROBLEM SHARED IS
A PROBLEM HALVED

I use my mouth A LOT. I am always chatting to people and discussing different ideas to help me understand life and happiness better. I love to talk and have learned over the years how it can make me feel really good.

Sometimes when we feel sad, we want to hide away and not talk to anyone. We may prefer to stay in bed and not tell anyone about the negative thoughts we are having. Yet I have learned that when I do talk about feelings I'm having, I feel much better afterwards. Telling someone else that you are having a tough time or that you feel sad about something can feel scary in the moment, but usually makes you feel calmer afterwards. This is because when we're all caught up in a worry or problem, it's hard to find the answers yourself. Asking someone who isn't involved in the problem can be all you need to get to grips with what you're feeling. There's a reason they say that a problem shared is a problem halved!

But I know it can be hard to get the words out of your mouth and ask for help when you feel sad. The words can feel a little bit like they are trapped in your throat and are fighting to stay in there. **But when we don't speak up and tell someone about how we are feeling, how can they know how to help?**

No matter what it is that's worrying you, it's usually best to talk to someone about it. You'll not only feel relieved that you've said the words out loud, but hopefully you'll also feel supported and like you have someone who can look out for you as they know you're having a tough time. Never feel scared to talk to someone who you love and trust if you are worried, scared, angry or sad. Let the words leave your mouth knowing that you'll feel much better afterwards.

So who can you speak to? It could be parents, carers, siblings, friends, teachers, or anyone else you trust. Remember, no matter how nervous you might feel, if you talk to someone you love or trust about your worries, your words will be met with kindness. Your loved ones are there to help you.

You can also use your mouth to help someone in need. If someone comes to you because they are having a tough time, you can use your words to help them feel supported. It's fantastic knowing that saying something kind to someone else can change their day for the better. Is there someone in your life, class or home who you think would love to chat to you? Do you have a friend or family member who needs some words of encouragement? Maybe you have a little brother or sister who is starting school and feels nervous and needs some comforting words. Or a friend who needs some advice. Remember how powerful words are. You can literally change someone's entire mood with them.

Here are some kind things you can say to someone you love that will make them feel good:

YOU ARE THE BEST

I THINK YOU ARE WONDERFUL

YOU ARE SOOOOOOO COOL

YOU'RE THE SMARTEST PERSON I KNOW

THANK YOU FOR ALWAYS BEING THERE FOR ME

THANK YOU FOR BEING YOU

YOU ARE THE GREATEST MATE EVER

And I'll let you into a little secret . . . you can also say these things to yourself! These statements are called affirmations and saying them out loud can help you feel better and more confident. If you repeat them over and over again, this helps your brain focus on them and ignore any negative thoughts. When I am feeling nervous about something, particularly when I need to speak in front of lots of people, I say out loud beforehand, 'I am happy and confident and everyone will enjoy what I'm going to say.' I may say this out loud four or five times to make sure my brain takes it on board!

If you are feeling a bit down you could say out loud to yourself,

I know the sadness will pass and I will be OK.

Or if you are feeling like you're struggling at school you could repeat to yourself,

I am clever and brilliant and I have so much to offer.

Say this four or five times to yourself and, even if you don't believe the words you are saying, know that they will still have an impact on how your brain and body react.

SMILE MORE!

Did you know that human teeth are just as strong as a shark's teeth? They might not be quite as big or pointy or sharp, but they are just as hard. How cool is that?

So isn't it time we show them off more?

The great thing about smiling is that – even if you're feeling down – if you force yourself to fake a smile it can make you feel a little happier. This has been proven by scientists! When you smile, your body releases those chemicals we spoke about earlier – **dopamine** and **endorphins** – which make you feel calmer and happier. Even if it feels like the smile isn't real, just the action of baring your teeth into a big grin tells your brain that you're feeling good, and tricks your body into releasing those happy hormones.

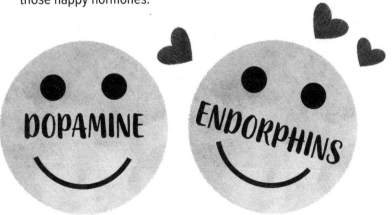

And not only that. When we see other people smile back at us it also makes us feel happy – it's almost like we catch their smile. So, when we fake smile at someone, we trick our body into feeling good. Then that person will smile back at us, which makes us feel even better. In no time at all, you'll be baring those shark teeth for real!

Why not see if you can start a smile chain today?

If you smile at one person, they might then feel a bit happier and smile at someone else, who then in turn feels happier and smiles at someone else, and so on! Think how far your smile chain could travel!

SMILING MORE
CAN MAKE THE
WHOLE WORLD

A HAPPIER PLACE!

HAPPY FOOD

As well as talking and smiling, the other great thing about mouths is that we can eat delicious food with them. Taste is another wonderful sense that can give us so much pleasure.

My happy food is peanut butter on toast. I like a thick piece of bread, toasted and slathered in butter and then peanut butter on top. When I bite into that thick, buttery toast I feel comforted and happy. Over the years I've worked out what flavours I love and what flavours I really can't stand. Are there any foods or flavours that you like or dislike?

Tasting our favourite foods can make us feel great, but it doesn't mean that eating them ALL the time will bring us joy. For example, many people love the taste of chocolate, but if you eat an entire chocolate cake, you will probably start to feel a little sick and not so happy an hour later. Chips are another food that taste amazing, but if we only ate chips for lunch, we would have very little energy for doing all the things we love later in the day. (On pages 164–165, we'll talk more about which foods can help our bodies feel energetic and which make us feel lazy and tired.)

So find your happy food – discover the flavours that explode in your mouth and fill you with joy. But just make sure you're careful with how much of your happy food you eat.

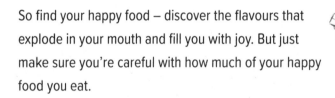

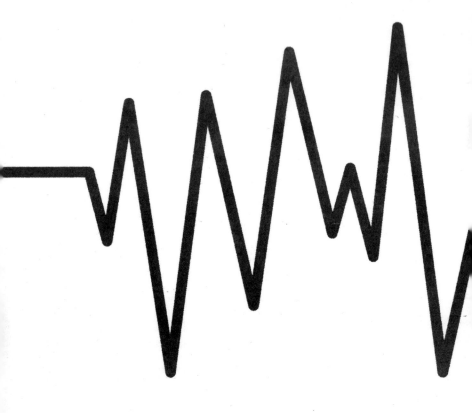

LISTEN UP

One of the first senses that comes into play when we are born is our hearing. We go from hearing muffled, comfortable, muted sounds in the womb to lots of different, very clear sounds the minute we are born.

Sounds are everywhere, but sometimes we take them for granted. We get used to certain noises – the bus driving past our house, the birds tweeting in the sky, the TV on in the next room. We can very rarely get away from them. Sometimes they can be a pain, and at other times they can be very soothing.

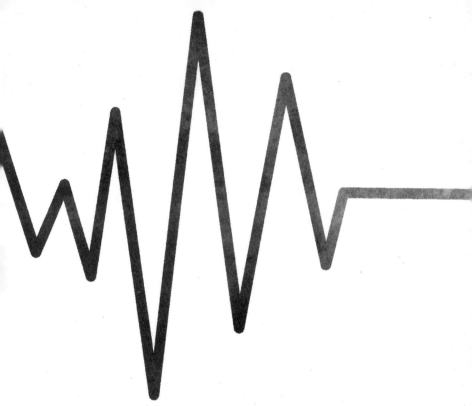

We very often *hear* noises, but we're not necessarily *listening* to them. My favourite sound is the sea rolling over the pebbles on a beach. It instantly makes me feel relaxed. I also love the sound of birds in the morning – their singing makes me very happy. When you find a sound you like, make sure you're truly listening and not treating it as background noise. Notice everything about the sound and really soak it all in. This can help you on your journey to feeling calm and joyful.

Piano music also makes me feel super chilled out. In fact, music can be the most powerful sound of all. Do you have a favourite song? A song that gets your toes tapping or your voice booming as you sing along? Or perhaps a song that makes you feel calm? Playing your favourite music can be a very good tool when you need an energy pick-me-up or a mood booster.

One thing you could do is create a happy playlist. Write down five to ten tracks that lift your mood whenever you listen to them. If you're able, you can then find these songs on YouTube and have a listen. Or if you don't have access to YouTube, share your list of happy songs with your family and ask if they'll play them and listen with you.

STRANGE SOUNDS

Sometimes I have trouble getting to sleep, and that's because I am picking up on the many sounds outside. I might be able to hear the bus that regularly passes my house, or people chatting on a late-night stroll with their barking dogs. On other occasions such as Fireworks Night, New Year's Eve or Diwali, I can hear loud fireworks booming in the sky. When noises distract me while I'm trying to sleep or get my work done, I try to think of them as just background noise. Rather than seeing them as a problem, I use my mind to let them fade into the background. I focus on my fingertips and put my attention on what they feel like when I press them together. Or I focus on my back pressing into the mattress and what that feels like. Choosing to focus on another sense can stop all the attention landing on the sound that's distracting you.

If that doesn't work, and I feel myself getting frustrated, I use earplugs, which you might find helpful too. In the daytime, if noises are distracting you while you are trying to concentrate, you could also try using a fidget toy so you can focus on the sensation of it in your hands rather than the noises around you.

Shhhhhh

At other times, noises might make us feel scared – especially at night – and then it's harder to make these sounds fade into the background. We might hear the radiator pop or someone next door walking up the stairs – this is when our imagination can run wild. But there are always going to be lots of noises constantly going on in the background in a home. If earplugs don't work, one thing that Rex and Honey find calming is called a white-noise machine. It gives off a constant *shhhhhh* sound that cancels out other noises at night-time and helps them fall asleep.

hhhhhhhhhh

SLEEP IS VERY
IMPORTANT
FOR ALLOWING
OUR BODIES TO
REST AFTER A
BUSY DAY, AND
ENSURES WE
WAKE UP
BRIGHT AND
READY TO FACE
THE NEXT DAY.

WHAT IS ADHD?

ADHD is a medical term given to people who either find it hard to concentrate, or experience hyperactivity and impulsiveness (meaning they may find it harder to stop themselves carrying out certain behaviours). It can also be a combination of both. But this doesn't mean there is anything wrong with people who have been diagnosed with it. It just might mean they need a little extra support to help them focus. School is full of distractions and lots of noises, and for children with ADHD, these noises can be even more distracting.

But if you have been diagnosed with ADHD, it's really nothing to worry about! In fact, I have been learning lots about ADHD recently and I sometimes wish I could remove the word 'disorder' from the name. I know a few people who have ADHD, and it seems to be more like a superpower than a disorder. At times it might be harder to focus on a task, which can be frustrating. But, for a person with ADHD, it might also mean that they have periods of time when they can focus with huge concentration on a subject or task they love. They can use tons of energy to create brilliant pieces of artwork, chunks of writing or cool and creative ideas. One of my friends who has ADHD is the most incredible painter, and he has learned to channel his energy into his art.

It really is a superpower.

If you want to find out more about ADHD, there is a website called kidshealth.org which I would recommend. If you search for ADHD on the website, you can learn more about the causes and signs of ADHD and what it feels like for kids who have it.

LISTENING TO OTHERS

Using our ears to listen to the people in our lives can be very valuable. For example, if you are worried about something, you can always turn to someone you trust for advice. Ask what they would do in your situation, then listen for their words of wisdom. They might have been in a similar situation previously, and have the experience to offer up some guidance that might help you. Listening to other people is a great way to learn and feel supported.

You can also use your ears to help someone in need. If you know that someone is upset, simply listening to them can make them feel much better. Helping someone else by listening not only makes the other person feel good, it makes you feel good too. You don't even have to come up with an answer or solution to their problem – often just lending them your ears is simply enough. It feels GREAT to be kind!

Why not practise your listening skills and ask a family member or friend a question to find out more about them? Really listen and try to learn something new about them and their life. It has to be something you didn't know already! Who will you choose to learn about?

LOVE YOUR FACE

Before we move on from the face and continue our journey through the human body, I'd love for you to meet my friend **Jono Lancaster**. He is a speaker and founder of a charity called Love Me, Love My Face Foundation. Jono was born with Treacher Collins Syndrome, which means he was born with no cheekbones, very small ears, and eyes that dip down. Jono was bullied as a child because of the way he looks, but over the years he learned to love himself and his brilliant face. He now travels the world helping other people – especially children who are born with Treacher Collins – to grow in confidence.

Jono Lancaster, speaker and charity founder

Jono, you're very passionate about faces and have even set up your own charity Foundation Love Me, Love My Face. Can you tell us about it?

Growing up, I never had the opportunity to connect with someone else that had a facial difference and I felt very alone and began to hate my face. Thankfully, I did reach a point where I began to love my face (and so much more about myself too). I believe I would have found that love at a much younger age if I had met someone just like me earlier. At Love My Face, we support patients, children, people and entire families with facial differences by connecting them to other families in similar situations and by hosting events. We also help with medical costs in certain cases. But, most importantly, we believe meeting other people just like you is really powerful and healing.

> # In that moment you get a feeling of 'I'm not the only one, I'm not alone.'

Can you remember meeting someone like yourself?
Yes, it's an instant bond. You don't even have to say
anything . . . but sooner rather than later, you're
saying it all. Nothing is off limits because they know
deeply what you mean in a way no one else can. You
end up sharing for hours (and years) and it doesn't
matter if you are from different races, or religions,
or cultures or backgrounds, as you have such a key
shared experience. Meeting someone like me makes
me feel seen and heard on a level that others can't
connect with. It's our own secret club and all secret
clubs are better with more members!

Can you teach us about Treacher Collins Syndrome?

It is a condition that people are born with; you don't catch it or develop it. It affects people in different ways, but it only affects the face. Some people have more severe cases and need dozens of surgeries to breathe, and others have relatively few surgeries, mostly to help them hear.

For me, my cheek bones haven't developed, so my eyes appear on a slant; my ears haven't fully developed, so I have these cool little ears that don't ever get cold in winter. I am partially deaf, so I wear a hearing aid that helps me to hear – and when I don't want to hear I can turn it off (as a child this came in very handy when my mum used to shout at me to do my homework)!

Sometimes Treacher Collins can also affect the airways, so some people require additional support to help them breathe, and some need a feeding tube to help them eat.

You've got a brilliant face which I know you're very fond of now, but that wasn't the case when you were a kid, was it?

As a kid I noticed that people would stare at me, others would point and laugh, and some called me nasty names. I never knew what to do in this situation. I was scared to tell an adult, embarrassed to tell friends, and I didn't want to hurt my mum by making her feel bad or stressed, so I kept that pain to myself and told no one. I used to look in the mirror that I had in my bedroom and cry for a face like everyone else.

Being a kid and growing up is tough; we all have things we're insecure about or wish were different.

BUT AS SOON AS WE REALIZE THOSE ARE OUR BEST QUALITIES THAT MAKE US UNIQUE, THE WORLD TRULY STARTS TO OPEN UP.

How did you start loving your face?

For years I tried to not look at my face, the mirror in my bedroom was covered up and I often looked at the floor, avoiding eye contact. This was my life up until I was twenty years old. My first moment of self-love came about by accident. I was working in a fitness centre where there were massive mirrors on every wall. Late one night I was clearing the weights up in front of one of these mirrors. I had some new trainers on and some short shorts and I couldn't help but admire the way I looked!

*I love my trainers, I thought.
I love my legs, I thought next.
I worked my way up my body,
admiring it, still smiling, then I
got to my face.*

For the first time in what felt like forever I saw my face. I stared at it; I noticed all my features and I was still smiling, not just a small smile though, but the biggest smile my face could possibly create. In that moment I said to myself:

I LOVE MY FACE!

What can people do if they feel shy, embarrassed or upset about their physical appearance?

When I look back at my life, one of the things I failed to do was speak up. I kept all my feelings inside when, in fact, I should have spoken to those around me. The process of forming the words helps your body understand all that jumble of feelings inside. I know speaking out is scary so writing things down can help! Writing is another way of your brain making sense of your feelings. You could write private notes or share them if you feel ready to do so. The more I've shared, the more I've loved, and this in turn has created so many magical moments and experiences with people from all walks of life, helping me to accept and celebrate my face.

What is your favourite part of your face?

This is a tough one between my blue eyes, my little ears and the one dimple that I have when I smile! But my favourite has to be my eyes: I love the colour, I love the shape, I love how they show my true feelings to those that get me.

What have you learned about faces over the years?

People are very good at using their faces to hide their true feelings and emotions. This makes it harder to have good relationships with yourself and others. When you start to show your true authentic self, the world magically opens up and starts to feel very real and beautiful.

I've also spent all my life admiring and at times being jealous of other faces. But I've learned that all faces have their own unique stamps on them and I think that's the best thing ever. I encourage everyone to celebrate their own unique face.

What makes you smile?

Simply seeing another smile – they're contagious. But also, people being kind to others with differences. It's one thing to be 'nice', but you can really change a life by including someone. Sometimes that just means listening to another person without judging them.

How can I love myself?

Treat yourself well. Eat nourishing foods, drink lots of water, wear clothes or colours that you like, clean yourself and your room, and move a little every day, even if it's just bopping your head to a song you like. These basics should be practised every day. Then, the next most important thing is to surround yourself with as many positive people as you can. And just remember

YOU CAN BE YOUR OWN BEST FRIEND AND YOUR OWN HERO. THE SOONER YOU LOVE YOURSELF, THE SOONER OTHERS WILL SEE THAT, AND THE RIGHT PEOPLE WILL BE DRAWN TO YOU.

We've now visited your whole head and your beautiful face. We've adventured into your amazing brain, moved around the different features of your face and looked at all the ways we can use these parts of our body to feel a little happier and make others feel happy too.

But the adventure has only just begun...

TOP TIPS
FOR A HAPPY FACE:

Look for the positives – they are all around you.

Think about what you're grateful for.

Find your happy colour.

Don't underestimate your nose – let smell calm you down and take you back to wonderful memories.

A problem shared is a problem halved.

Spread kindness with your words.

Make a happy playlist.

Remember that your face is unique and that's what makes you special.

Smile as much as you can.

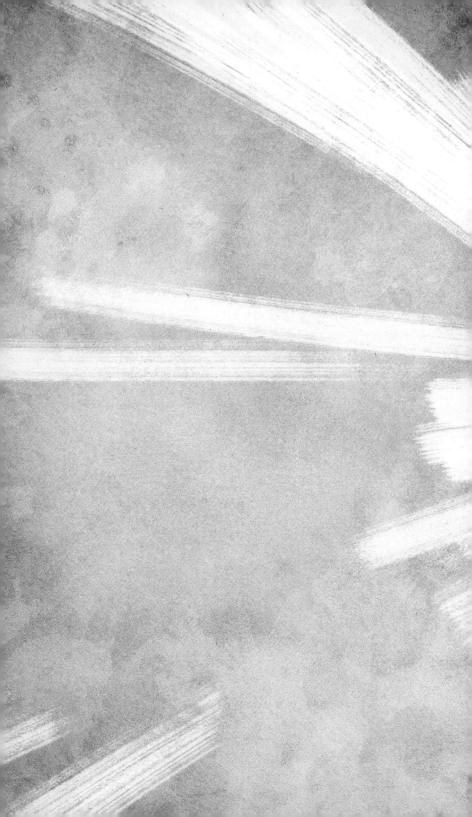

CHAPTER 3

Unbelievable upper body

STAND LIKE A SUPERHERO

As we move down our neck, the next body part we come to is our shoulders. Notice how your shoulders are sitting today. Are they slumped? Is your back curved or straight? If you have been at school all day and only had break-times to stand up and move around, you might notice your back is a little curved, or that your shoulders are slouching forward slightly.

Imagine a piece of string is pulling you from the top of your head. Imagine each vertebra – the small bones in your back that make up your spine – is stretching out, giving the one below it more room. Let your back straighten, but make sure your shoulders don't rise up – keep them dropped down away from your neck and ears. Does that feel better? It's important to check in with your back regularly and give it a good stretch. I think you might have just grown a few centimetres there!

The way your shoulders are positioned can change the entire way your body feels. I'm going to let you into a little secret – a tip for how you can feel powerful, even when deep inside you might be feeling worried. Try this now: walk out of the room you are in, then walk back in with your shoulders slumped and your face staring at the floor. How did it make you feel? A little down in the dumps? Less confident? Now do the same thing again, only this time walk in with your back straight and your head held up high. How did that feel? A little sunnier?

Maybe you felt more confident or powerful?

THE POWER POSE

Recently I had to go and do a talk in front of lots of people, and I was feeling very nervous about it. I was scared I might mess up my words or trip over on the stage. Feeling nervous when speaking in public is completely normal, but my friend taught me a new trick I've since used lots of times. It's called the power pose and is backed up by real science. Here's how you do it:

1. *Stand with your legs slightly apart from each other.*

2. *Push your shoulders back.*

3. *Lift your head up.*

4. *Place your arms either on your hips or held high in the air above your head in the shape of the letter V.*

5. *Stay like this for a whole minute.*

It feels like a long time, and if your arms are above your head you might even start to get pins and needles a little. After one minute of the power pose, you'll hopefully be feeling a lot more confident about whatever it is that you're nervous about. And that is thanks to the amazing power of science.

Remember how linked your body and brain are? Well, holding this pose for one minute allows your brain to catch up with how your body is feeling. For that minute, you are making your body language say 'I am here, and I am ready.' Your brain then picks up on this and starts to feel more positive and confident. So give it a go the next time you have a nerve-wracking task ahead – it's hard to still feel nervous or shy when you're in the power pose.

I AM HERE,
I AM READY

BODY LANGUAGE

The way your shoulders are positioned can also impact what people think about you. We all know what language means: choosing the right words in the right order to express yourself. But did you know that we also respond not only to words, but other people's posture and movements too? This is called body language, and this unspoken language allows us to let others know how we are feeling by the way we move and hold our bodies. If you are moving quickly or fidgeting, others will know you're excited or nervous. If you're moving slowly and looking towards the floor, others can assume you are tired or feeling shy or upset.

If you saw somebody standing with their shoulders hunched over, picking at the skin on their fingers, with their head turned down towards the floor and their legs tightly wound together, how do you think they would be feeling? Probably nervous, down or upset about something. If you saw someone standing with their shoulders pushed back and their spine straight, with their head held high and their hands on their hips, how would you say they might be feeling? I would say powerful.

YOUR BODY
CAN SPEAK A
THOUSAND WORDS
WITHOUT YOU
EVEN SAYING A
THING. SO IF YOU
WANT PEOPLE
TO KNOW THAT
YOU'RE FEELING
GREAT – SHOW
THEM WITH YOUR
SHOULDERS!

UNDERSTANDING AUTISM

Autism is a disability that can affect how people experience the world. One in 100 people are on the autism spectrum. Some autistic people need a lot of support with day to day activities, but others might only need a little bit of help.

Like everyone in the world, autistic people have things they like and are good at, as well as things they struggle with. For autistic people, picking up on body language cues can be tricky, as they might have difficulties understanding people's feelings, language and body language. Bright lights and loud noises may also feel very uncomfortable, and it might take longer to understand instructions or take in information.

If you are someone who doesn't struggle with these things, then it's still important to understand autism so you can help others who might need extra support feel safe and settled.

Just remember that everyone is different.

Every single person in the world is unique and we need to respect each other's differences and try to understand others as much as we can. If you want to know more about autism, there are some great books you can read, such as *A Different Sort of Normal* by Abigail Balfe, plus some additional resources at the back of this book.

HEART OF JOY

Now let's move down the torso a little towards your heart. Put your hand over it now. If you're not sure where it is, move your hand down from your neck to the top of your ribcage, then move it over a little to the left. There, that's it. You should be able to feel your heart beating. The speed at which it beats will change depending on what you're doing. After doing any sports, you will probably find that your heart is beating very fast – that's because it's having to work extra hard to pump blood all around your body to the muscles as they move.

Keeping your heart happy and healthy is important for a happy mind. You can do this by eating nutritious food and moving your body regularly. Exercise can change your mood massively. When you move your body, those feel-good chemicals called endorphins are released and make you feel great. We'll talk more about exercise on pages 204–206, where we'll discover more about how movement can not only improve your heart health, but also put a smile on your face.

LOTS OF LOVE

When we think about the heart, we also tend to think about love. I love my children and my husband, and luckily I see them every day. But I also have great friends who live in different countries, so it's difficult to be together regularly. I enjoy sending postcards and letters, as well as emails and text messages, to those I love who don't live near me. I feel more connected to them, and it's always fun receiving a letter back in the post. Rex has a good friend called Lennon who lives in another country, and they frequently write letters to each other too. I also love our twenty-year-old cat, Keloy, who brings the whole family so much joy.

Who do you love? Grab a pen and paper, and write down one to three names of people who give you that warm, loving feeling when you think about them. This list might change over time, so do update it whenever you need to. Having a little list of people you love can act as a valuable reminder that you're never alone.

As well as having this support system of friends and relatives that you love, it's also very important to love yourself. That might sound like a funny thing to say, but it's something we can forget to do quite easily. Let me explain. If you find that you're comparing yourself to friends, or if you get told off at school, it is easy to think badly of yourself. You might feel like you are not good enough in some way, or that you always seem to get things wrong.

REMEMBER: WE ARE HUMANS, NOT ROBOTS. WE ARE ALL GOING TO GET THINGS WRONG SOMETIMES.

I'm TERRIBLE at maths – I can't even do Rex's homework when he needs help. But rather than feeling bad and telling myself I'm not good enough, I choose to have compassion for myself. I remember that although I might not be so good at maths, I do love to write so am always on hand when Rex has tricky English homework to complete. I'm also good at art, which allows us all to have creative fun as a family. By concentrating on the things I know I'm good at, I don't have time to dwell on the fact that I'm not so skilled when it comes to maths. In that moment I've chosen to be kind to myself and remember my strengths. I treat myself like I would a best friend. Compassion is a bit like love – it means caring for others or yourself, rather than judging or putting yourself or others down.

Loving yourself and celebrating your achievements is very important when it comes to overall happiness. Keep in mind that you might be jealous of someone else, but everyone has their own insecurities and it's likely that there's something you have that they might be jealous of too! Comparing yourself to other people will never make you feel good.

JUST REMEMBER – YOU ARE BRILLIANT.

DOING THINGS YOU LOVE

Spending time doing activities you love with people you love can really help to boost your mood. As a family, we really enjoy having a movie night. We buy our favourite snacks, choose a film that everyone will enjoy, then get into our pyjamas and snuggle down for the night.

Think of five things you have done recently with friends, family or people you love.

It could be . . .

A DAY AT THE PARK

PLAYING BOARD GAMES IN YOUR HOUSE

LOOKING AT OLD PHOTOS WITH A RELATIVE

A VISIT TO THE CINEMA

A TRAIN JOURNEY

A TRIP TO THE BEACH

DOING ARTS AND CRAFTS

If these memories made you smile, can you make any time to do more of those things? Maybe ask a parent or carer if you can have a family day trip, or see if it's possible to invite your best mate over after school for some time to do your favourite activity together.

TURNING HOBBIES INTO SKILLS

Sometimes you'll find that when you love doing a hobby or activity, you get very good at it. This is because repetition helps your brain and body improve a skill. For example, if you love playing the piano and keep going back to it, you're likely to get better at it over time. If you adore drama club and go every week you'll hopefully notice over time that you get more confident too. I love writing and have got better at it with each book I write.

But being the best at something isn't the only important thing. Just because my first attempts at writing might not have been as well structured or as easy to write as the books I'm writing now, it doesn't mean they're less important. When we are starting out with a new hobby or skill, we have to remember the most important part of the process is that we enjoy it, rather than only focusing on getting good at it. That part should just happen naturally!

I have a friend who loves what he does so much that his hobbies have become his actual job! And you might know him too. **Tom Fletcher**'s love of playing the guitar, singing and composing songs for years as a kid led him to form a band called McFly, tour the world and release lots of music that brought tons of people joy. He has now turned his love of writing into another part of his job, as he also writes **BRILLIANT** books. Have you ever read *The Christmasaurus*? Let's find out more from Tom about his love of writing, and how following his passion makes him feel.

Tom Fletcher, songwriter and author

Tom, you write books (we're all huge fans of *The Christmasaurus* in my house), write and play music, and create stage shows. What do you love the most?

I think I get the same excitement and satisfaction from all of them, but ultimately I'm always drawn back to music. Nothing quite touches my emotions like music, and writing a song is a pretty wonderful, unique feeling.

How old were you when you realized you loved music?

Younger than I can remember! My dad sings and plays guitar, so there was always music in my house when I was little and my first experiences of singing onstage were with him and his band when I was only four or five. I've loved it ever since.

A song can make you feel a whole range of emotions – that's the beauty of music. When you need a pick-me-up you can go to your happy song, or perhaps you need something to help you to relax or even be the soundtrack to your tears when you need a cry. There's always a song for you.

When you're doing something you love, how does it make you feel?
It's almost so good that you can't even appreciate it until after it's over. I think my best experiences of performing live – or even writing a song – have come when I've been totally in the moment, not thinking about what I want to have for dinner after the show or the thing that upset me just before. Just being PRESENT with no distractions.

Do you think you have to be good at something to enjoy it?
Hahahahaha! NO WAY! I'm genuinely a TERRIBLE pianist, a very average guitarist and my voice sounds

like a wasp stuck in a trumpet . . . but when I'm doing those things onstage, I'm too busy having the time of my life to care!

Not being 'good' comes with some frustrations sometimes, such as when my lack of skill or talent prevents me from doing something I want to. But luckily I've surrounded myself with people who are WAY better than I am, so I can just enjoy myself while learning and improving all the time!

How does it feel to know that other people love reading your books and listening to your music?
I absolutely love that what I write is enjoyed by people! It makes me really happy. But actually I get my main dose of happiness BEFORE anyone has ever heard or read anything, when I'm in the middle of writing and creating it. For me it's about the journey, not the destination. I don't ever want to let my happiness or enjoyment of something rely on other people's opinions, as they are out of my control. I find enjoyment in the process of creating it.

Tom has discovered what he loves and has learned that it doesn't matter what other people think about it. His main focus is enjoying the task at hand, which is the part he finds fun and stimulating.

REMEMBER: IT DOESN'T MATTER WHAT OTHERS THINK ABOUT YOUR HAPPY HOBBY – DO IT BECAUSE YOU LOVE IT!

FIND YOUR THING

If you're not sure what you love to do, it's time to get experimenting so you can work out what your happy hobby is. Don't worry if yours is different from your friends' – if all your classmates love football, but you like going to a karate class it doesn't matter one bit. If all your friends love collecting Pokémon cards but you prefer reading wildlife books then that's completely OK.

If your friends don't understand that you have different interests, try speaking to them about why you love your happy hobby so much. Explain how it makes you feel and why you've chosen to concentrate on it, rather than doing the same as everybody else.

The most important thing is that you choose an activity or hobby that makes YOU feel good. Think how boring it would be if we all liked the same stuff! Every single person will have something individual to them that makes them happy. It is completely different for everyone. Each one of us is unique, and that's something to celebrate. You might even encourage your friends to try something new too.

AND BREATHE ...

Inside your ribcage – the hard bones that protect your chest and support your upper torso – you'll find your lungs, which are two of the most important features of your brilliant body. Without you having to think about it, your lungs are working away all day, causing you to inhale (breathe in) and exhale (breathe out).

Take one deep breath in now and watch how your chest rises as your lungs expand. Now release all the air you've just breathed in and watch your chest sink back down again as your lungs deflate. That's happening all day long without you even realizing!

Do you know why breathing is so important? When you breathe in, your lungs absorb oxygen from the air and transfer it to your blood, which then travels all around your body, delivering oxygen to all your cells. Along the way, your blood collects a waste gas called carbon dioxide, which it then takes back to the lungs to be exhaled,. You are quite literally breathing in the good stuff and breathing out the bad stuff! But how can you use your breath to help you feel happier and calmer?

FEELING SCARED

We've already talked a lot about those moments when your breath moves in and out of your body quicker than it might normally. It might be because you're doing something active, like playing sports. It might also be because you're doing something thrilling, which makes you feel scared, like if you're on a roller coaster. And, as we talked about before, your imagination can be so powerful that, even when you simply think about something scary, your body reacts as though you're really experiencing that thing.

Think about the last time you felt nervous. You might have noticed yourself breathing more quickly. Although this is a natural reaction to nerves, the quick breaths can actually make us feel more nervous and scared. It's like our lungs and brain are connected and are having a conversation with each other.

Imagine how that might go:

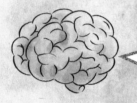

I don't want to stand up and tell my story to the class. Public speaking makes me nervous.

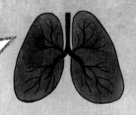

Did someone say public speaking? **OH NO**. I think we should start breathing a little quicker now to prepare you for it.

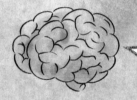

I'm struggling to breathe normally, which must mean I'm really nervous. And any minute now I'm going to have to speak in front of everyone. **HELP.**

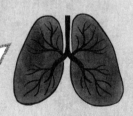

Help? OK, I'll do what I can to help your body prepare! Let's breathe really quickly now, with short, sharp breaths . . .

Well, now I feel even worse. I'm not taking in any air at all, which means I'm not oxygenating my body properly. I really feel like I'm in danger now. **SLOW DOWN!**

The more we panic, the faster we breathe, and the faster we breathe, the more we panic. So what can we do? It's a bit like the question 'What came first: the chicken or the egg?' Do we tell our brain to stop worrying in order to slow down our breathing, or do we try to slow down our breathing to help our brain stop worrying? How can we help ourselves calm down?

Well – unlike the chicken-and-egg situation – there is a clear answer here! It's actually much harder to tell your brain to stop worrying than to control your breathing. As we have discovered, our brains are complex and sometimes a little rebellious. They can ignore our wishes and run wild when we tell them to calm down.

When it comes to your lungs, you have much more control over them, so you can tell them what to do with a little more ease. In those moments when you feel nervous or panicked, try working on your breathing first. Just think about the air going into your lungs as you take one **LONG** breath in and then imagine all the air leaving your lungs as you **SLOWLY** breathe out again. After a minute or so of doing this, you will hopefully notice your brain is worrying less as you are focusing on your breath. You might also notice that by breathing slowly your heart rate has slowed down too, making you feel even calmer (and hopefully a little happier).

Please remember that being nervous sometimes is totally normal, and there is nothing wrong with feeling that way occasionally. But hopefully some careful and mindful breathing will help you in those moments.

My friend **Rebecca Dennis** knows ALL about the power of breathing. Rebecca is a breath coach and it is her job to help people to breathe well and to feel happier.

Hey, Rebecca, as someone who has studied breathing for many years, can you tell us a little bit about it?

Breathing is a superpower, and just because we breathe automatically every day doesn't mean we should take it for granted! The average person takes around 20,000 breaths a day. Most people can hold their breath for a maximum of one to two minutes, but in 2010 a Danish freediver named Stig Severinsen held his breath underwater for an extraordinary twenty-two minutes. (A freediver is someone who holds their breath underwater for long periods of time rather than relying on an oxygen tank.)

Breathing is a simple, natural thing we do each day. It's the thing we can't stop doing because it is what keeps us alive.

> # Your emotions can change the way you breathe and the way you breathe can change your emotions.

It is our breath that changes when we see someone we love; when we get nervous; when we are happy. It is the thing that helps us become calm when we feel anxious or scared.

If you watch a little baby breathing while it's asleep, you will notice their WHOLE body looks like it is breathing – the breath moves almost like an ocean wave. But as we grow up we stop using our whole breathing system, and we tend to only use a third of it. But, in fact, babies are expert breathers and we have a lot to learn from them!

Some of us become chest breathers, while others breathe more in the belly. Some only take shallow breaths or regularly hold their breath. By opening the breath and practising breathwork we can breathe more freely and enjoy life even more!

Just as you are taught to brush your teeth, tidy your room, bathe, talk, say 'please' and 'thank you', you should also learn to practise breathwork because of all its incredible benefits.

How can noticing our breathing patterns help us?
Psychologists and researchers have discovered that breathwork can help reduce negative thoughts, and help people to feel less anxious and stay focused. Practising breathwork is a life-long tool for managing emotions, improving physical performance, boosting self-confidence, building mental strength and feeling happier within yourself. Each and every one of us has the ability to use our breath to feel calmer, more relaxed and more alert at any given moment. Breathing properly can also help to reduce your blood pressure. This is a good thing as it improves your cardiovascular fitness, meaning you can exercise for longer without running out of steam.

How can we discover our breathing pattern?

As you breathe, start to follow the inhale and exhale and pick up all the information you can gather. Notice the rise and fall of the inhale and exhale. Place one hand on your belly and one hand on your chest and see which one rises first.

How fast is your breathing? How full is your breathing? Where does the movement start and finish? Can you stay focused on the breath and bring all your awareness to the breath you take in and then the one you breathe out? Can you feel the breath moving more in your tummy or your chest, or is it equal in both?

What happens to our bodies when we slow down our breath?

Bringing breathwork into the day at mealtimes, bedtime or on the way to school helps you to notice how different breathing exercises affect how you feel. By simply taking the time to pause and be aware of your breath, you create healthy habits.

Taking short, quick breaths when you feel anxious and upset actually makes those feelings worse. These breaths can increase dizziness, stop you from being able to think straight, make your heart race and more. Slowing down the breath sets off a chain of responses in the body that bring in feelings of calm and relaxation.

The best tip I can give you is:

BE MORE LIKE
A TORTOISE.

A tortoise breathes just four times a minute and can live to be well over one hundred years old. I'm not saying that changing your breathing will definitely help you live to one hundred, but we could all do with being more like a tortoise. Slowing down your breath can help you let go of racing thoughts and bring stillness and calm to your body and mind.

What's a good breathing pattern to get into if we want to feel calmer or happier?

Breathing into your belly will immediately help if you are feeling a bit stuck and need to gather your thoughts. The diaphragm is a muscle that sits under your ribcage, and deep belly breaths help you exercise this muscle. This will fill you with energy and also make you feel calm and focused.

Practise this exercise with a smile on your face. Start

by thinking of the emotion you are feeling right now. Is it fear? Anger? Nerves? Keep thinking of that feeling and then take some deep breaths focusing on that emotion. Don't try to push the feeling away – just let it hang around for as long as it needs to while you calmly breathe. This will help to naturally move the feeling on. Then:

- Stand up straight with your arms by your side and feet about hip-width apart.

- Inhale and expand your belly for a count of five while lifting your arms up to the sky.

- Hold your breath for a count of five and relax into that hold.

- Then, exhale for a count of five while lowering the arms.

- Repeat this a few times and notice how you feel afterwards.

Can breathing in a certain way help us fall asleep at night?

If you are having trouble sleeping, being aware of your breath will help you relax and fall asleep.

While you sleep, your body produces hormones that help you grow and feel happy.

A GOOD NIGHT'S SLEEP INCREASES ATTENTION SPAN AND EVEN HELPS IMPROVE YOUR PERFORMANCE AT SCHOOL!

In general, you will be more active and more alert after a good night's sleep.

So here's something you can try if you're finding it hard to fall asleep at night:

- Lie down on your bed and get comfy.

- Inhale for a count of four, hold for a count of seven.

- Then exhale for a count of eight.

- Close your eyes and bring your focus to your feet and toes.

- Continue to breathe in for four, hold for seven and exhale for eight.

- Continue working up the rest of your body, focusing on one body part at a time all the way to the top of your head. Keep your eyes closed as you continue to breathe in that same pattern.

What breathing exercise should we try when we feel stressed?

When you are feeling overwhelmed or finding it hard to gather your thoughts, this soothing exercise might help you to feel safe. This is great for when it's exam time, or you are finding it hard to focus or switch off. It can help you stay alert and calm at the same time. This box breath is simple and easy to do anytime when you feel strong emotions.

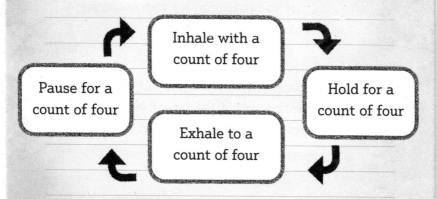

Is there a breathing exercise that can help you feel happier in yourself?

This next exercise helps you connect to the breath, be compassionate to your body and be kinder to yourself and others.

Be curious and enjoy it!

- Sit down on the floor or on your bed.

- Take a pause to slow down a little and notice your body and breath.

- Relax your belly and take a few slower breaths into your belly.

- Move your shoulders and neck round, allowing yourself to experience all the different sensations within your body.

- Begin to massage your feet and toes while breathing slowly, and then massage your calves and legs.

- Acknowledge your feelings with curiosity. Ask yourself, *'What am I feeling right now?'*

- Think about your feet, calves, hips and belly, chest and throat and notice any sensations in these areas.

- Massage your right arm slowly by gently squeezing the muscles from the shoulder down to your elbow with your left hand, and then down to your hand. Repeat on the left side.

- Notice which thoughts are present in your mind, but make sure you are being kind and compassionate towards yourself.

- Keep staying with the breath and notice how you feel. Rather than trying to push emotions away, sit with them and be with them.

Breathing really is your superpower. Everyone can do it, and we all now have the knowledge to help us use it in the most positive way.

Remember: using your breath and your lungs is a fantastic way to feel happier and calmer from top to toe.

TOP TIPS

FOR A HAPPY
UPPER BODY:

Find the people you love and spend time with them.

Find a happy hobby.

Check in with your breathing and use it to find calmness.

Love yourself and celebrate your achievements.

Remember that everyone is different and unique in their own way.

Stand like a superhero to feel more confident.

CHAPTER 4

Your brilliant belly

Let's now move a little further down the body to your tummy. Place your hands on yours and think about how it feels. Some are beautifully squidgy and stick out a little bit (mine does), and some feel flatter and harder. Some are enormous as they are growing a baby inside.

Although everyone's tummy looks a little different, they all have similar stuff going on inside – and there is A LOT going on! Inside this part of your body you have your stomach, which is where your food arrives after you've swallowed it; your intestines, which are long wiggly tubes that help pass your food through your body and out the other end as poo; your kidneys, which remove waste and fluid from your body; your liver, which cleans your blood and helps with digestion; and your bladder, where all your wee is stored before you go to the toilet. And the most extraordinary thing is how this is all just happening without you having to tell your body what to do!

Sometimes people need a little help with some of those bodily functions. Some people wear a stoma bag, which is a small bag attached to the outside of their tummy that collects poo from their bodies. They will have had a stoma bag fitted due to either illness or injury that has prevented poo from travelling down to exit out of their bum. A stoma bag is quite small and discreet and wearers can still run, walk, dance and do all the things they love.

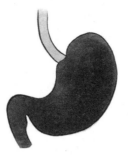

THE STOMACH

We chatted earlier about how some foods feel great to eat, how some boost our brains and how others make us feel bad or tired. We're now going to chat to my friend **Rhiannon Lambert**, who is a registered nutritionist and author. She's going to explain how food and mood are connected.

Does food affect our mood?

Yes! A healthy and balanced diet can change the way we think and feel and can improve our everyday mood. The food we choose to eat can also help with sleep and concentration. Scientists have recently discovered that our brain and our digestive system may be linked by something called the gut–brain axis. This means that our brain and gut are always talking to each other. We know that the brain affects our gut because we often feel butterflies in our tummy when we are upset, nervous or excited, but we also now know that what we eat can affect our brain health.

What is gut health and why does it matter when it comes to feeling good?

The gut runs from our mouth all the way to our bottom, and is where our food goes to be broken down and absorbed by the body. It is made up of millions and millions of tiny living things known as bacteria. They help the body to break down and absorb all the food we eat so that we are getting the right amount of nutrients that are important for good health. The key to a healthy gut is how many different types of these bacteria you have in your tummy – the more good bacteria you have, the better your gut health. These good bacteria feed off the food we eat, especially fibre. Fibre is found in lots of foods like **fruits** and **vegetables**, **carbohydrates**, **nuts** and **seeds**, and other **plant foods**.

Good gut health is important because our gut plays a huge role in making us feel great. For example, the body's

happy hormone (serotonin)
is made via the gut. So it is
important that we keep our
gut healthy to keep our
mind healthy too. Most of
our immune system (which
is the part of our body
that helps us when we are poorly)
is also found in the gut. So by looking after
our gut, we are giving our body the best chance of
fighting off any illness.

Which foods help us to boost our moods?

- Fruits and vegetables.
- Proteins such as oily fish (like salmon), chicken, eggs, tofu, nuts and seeds.
- Wholegrains and plant foods, such as beans and brown pasta.

What are processed foods and why are they not good for our health?

Processed foods are foods which have been changed in some way to make them taste or feel different or to make them last longer. They can lower the variety of good bacteria found in your gut. However, not all processed food is bad for our health, for example, frozen and tinned fruits and vegetables and tinned fish and beans are processed, but these are important parts of a balanced diet. Some foods are called ultra-processed foods, such as sweets, crisps and cakes. We need to eat less of these foods because they have high fat, salt and sugar levels, which isn't good for your gut if you have too much of them.

What are your favourite feel-good foods and why do you like to cook them?

For breakfast, I love a big bowl of porridge as you can top it with lots of exciting things like figs, peanut butter, yoghurt or berries. I also love pancakes as I can get creative with flavours. My favourite kinds are banana and oat pancakes but I love savoury ones too, like spinach and ricotta. Low-sugar banana bread is also a delicious snack that I enjoy baking with my family!

Have you noticed which foods make you feel happy AND give you energy? Have you noticed which ones make you feel sluggish and sleepy? Noticing how your body reacts to different foods can be really helpful. It will tell you which foods you should eat more of because they lift your mood and make your body feel good, and which you might want to have less of.

Here are some foods that I know make me feel GREAT:

PEANUT BUTTER. I love any nut butter – cashew, almond, peanut! They're all delicious on oatcakes, toast, on top of porridge or scooped up with slices of apple. Nut butters are high in fibre and protein, so they give you lots of long-lasting energy.

SWEET POTATOES. They are delicious, there is so much you can do with them, AND they are also packed full of vitamins and minerals.

WE GO BANANAS FOR BANANAS IN OUR HOUSE! We get through at least two bunches a week. My favourite thing to do with bananas is freeze them and then blend them into creamy smoothies. They're so tasty, and full of potassium, which helps to keep your heart working efficiently.

SPINACH. I find it very tasty cooked with oil and garlic in a pan, or a great way to get spinach and all its nutrients into your system is to add frozen blocks of it to smoothies. Spinach gives me loads of energy and makes me feel very happy indeed.

FARTS AND POO

I LOVE chocolate, and sometimes I can't stop myself eating too much of it – but then half an hour or so later, I notice it looks a bit like I've got a basketball hidden under my T-shirt, and sometimes it even feels a little painful too. That's because my stomach is bloated and full of air.

IT'S TIME TO TALK FARTS AND POO! COME ON, WE ALL DO IT!

The clever thing about poo is that it can very handily give us information about how we're feeling. Our tummy is a place that is connected to lots of emotions, and if we are feeling excited or nervous our tummy is often where we will physically feel it first.

Let me give you an example. Last week I felt stressed – I had a lot of work to get done, and a lot of things to do for my family and around the house. I felt as though time was running out, and that I wouldn't manage to do all of those jobs on my list. As we've found out, when we are stressed, it's not just our thoughts that can be affected – our body reacts to the stress too. I could feel that the muscles in my back were very tense, and my tummy felt a little painful. When your body feels like this, you may notice you poo less. You might not be able to go to the toilet at all, or maybe you do small, hard pellets of poo like a rabbit. This is called constipation and it can make you feel very grumpy and irritable. It's actually very clever really, as it's your poo trying to tell you something. The conversation might go a little like this:

POO: *Hey, I'm stuck in here. I can't get out.*

YOU: *I know. Sorry about that. My muscles are feeling tense and I have a lot on my mind.*

POO: *Could you try to find some time to relax or do something that makes you happy?*

YOU: *How is that going to help?*

POO: *Well, it just means that the body will stop creating the stress hormone (cortisol), which is not helping in the 'me-getting-out-of-here' department.*

YOU: *OK, well, I love drawing and it usually makes me feel calm so maybe I could try that . . .*

POO: *Yes, PLEASE. Anything to make you feel less stressed and happier will help get me out of here.*

As frustrating as constipation is, you just have to remember that it's your body's way of telling you to take some time out to calm down. Doing something that makes you feel relaxed will help your brain and muscles relax too. This will mean we can poo with more ease, sleep better and feel happier.

However, things can go the other way too. When we are nervous about something, our poo might be runnier than normal and also want to come out several times a day. In my family, we call this a 'funny tummy'. If you have a funny tummy, the best thing to do is let your parent or carer know, so they can look after you and feed you the best foods to get your belly feeling better.

And remember: it's completely normal. Everyone poos — even the Queen!

SLOW IT DOWN

Many people believe that our tummy is like a second brain. As well as being aware of WHAT you are eating, the tummy is also aware of HOW you are eating.

Do you rush your meals as you are desperate to leave the table and do something else? When we eat too quickly and don't chew enough times, the food travelling down our food pipe – or our **oesophagus**, to use the fancy scientific name for it – is not broken down properly, so our stomach has to work even harder when the food arrives there. This might give you a strange feeling in your tummy – or even in your chest area – called indigestion. This is your body telling you to slow down.

One way to slow down is to practise mindfulness while you're eating. Mindful eating involves really paying attention to what you are eating, and focusing on the flavours and textures of the food. This will encourage you to eat more slowly, enjoy your food and help to avoid indigestion. Taking your time allows you to notice how delicious the food actually is.

SOOTHING THE STOMACH

In those moments when your tummy (or any other body part for that matter) is trying to tell you something, there is a trick you can try. This works particularly well if your stomach is hurting because you're nervous about something:

1. Sit or lie down somewhere comfortable.
2. Place your hands over your stomach.
3. Imagine your favourite colour.
4. Now imagine that colour coming gently out of your hands and into your belly.
5. Imagine the colour feels warm and comforting, and picture it soothing your tummy and all that is going on inside it.

You can use your imagination to picture energy beaming out of your hands like you're a superhero, straight into any part of your body that needs soothing!

We've travelled through your upper body now. We have learned how the tummy is cleverly communicating with your body, and how the food you eat and your mood are linked. We've also learned some amazing tips and tricks when it comes to breathing. I think it's time to travel across to your arms!

TOP TIPS
FOR A HAPPY BELLY:

Eat food that makes you feel good.

Try eating mindfully.

If you're having digestion problems, do something that makes you feel relaxed.

Don't be embarrassed about poo – even the Queen does it!

Imagine you're a superhero, soothing your stomach!

CHAPTER 5

Arms and hands

HIGH

Think of all the incredible things you can do with your arms and hands. You're probably using them right now to hold this book! Not only can your hands be used to help you feel happier, they can also very quickly let other people know whether you are happy or not.

Do you remember when I told you right at the start of this book that I chat to many interesting people from all over the world about our brains and bodies? Well, I spoke to one author called Mel Robbins recently who has written a brilliant book called *The High 5 Habit*. When I interviewed Mel she taught me all about the power of high-fiving. When someone high-fives you, it can make you feel happy and

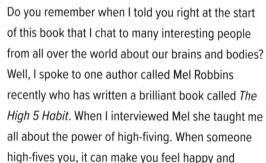

FIVE!

aware that the other person feels happy too. If a teacher high-fives you, it can make you feel like you are doing well and they have noticed, which feels great. Imagine if you could have that feeling every day. Well, Mel says you can. She advises that every morning when you wake up, you give yourself a high five in the mirror. In that moment you'll feel like you've just told yourself that you are doing well and are acknowledging all the brilliant things about yourself. It's a really positive way to start your day. Whether you do it first thing in the morning, after a sports match or an exam at school, or whenever you feel like you just want to congratulate yourself, pop in front of a mirror and give yourself a high five. It's a little gesture to give yourself a well-deserved boost.

HANDY HANDS

We can all use our hands to help people understand how we are feeling. When I talk, my hands are usually flailing about at the same time, helping to tell a story as I'm speaking. If I'm talking about something that excites me, my hand gestures will be big and dramatic. If I am talking about something upsetting, or feeling nervous, I might be clasping my hands together or fiddling with my nails as I speak. If I am angry I might wave my arms in the air, or if I am happy or have just received great news I might punch the air with joy. When we are in social situations, it is important to try to understand the people around us and how they are feeling. As well as listening to their words, we can pick up clues by watching how their hands move. Next time you have a conversation, watch how the other person moves their hands when they are talking. It will give you some great clues as to how they are really feeling, and will help you understand how to communicate with them. For example, if someone is clearly feeling nervous, you can be compassionate and gentle in the way you speak to them.

Hands can be a very important tool for so many people in ways we often don't realize. Some people rely on their hands to communicate with others through sign language. Sign language uses a series of shapes and movements made with your hands, which relate to different letters and words. If somebody has trouble hearing, or belongs to the Deaf community, they might use their hands to create signs to communicate with other people and let them know how they are feeling. And just like there are many different languages across the world, there are different forms of sign language depending on which country you live in. Below are the signs for each letter of the alphabet, in British Sign Language. Why not find the letters that make up your name and try to spell it?

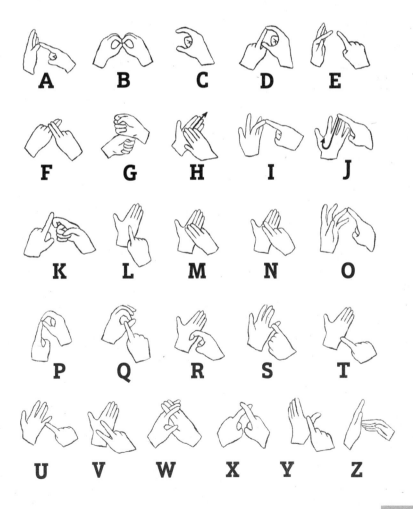

GET CR

There are so many more exciting and creative things you can do with your hands. I love to paint, so one of my favourite ways to use my hands is to pick up my paintbrushes and get to work on a colourful painting.

Getting creative can help with happiness in lots of ways. Not only is it fun, but it can also help you express emotions that you might not know how to talk about with words. If you are feeling sad or scared about something, expressing yourself creatively can really help to release those feelings. You could draw pictures that represent how you are feeling, write a story

EATIVE

or even dance like no one's watching! If you want to share a drawing or story with someone who you think could help you, then you might find this easier than talking. But, also, getting creative can just be the perfect way to let loose, enjoy yourself and create whatever you want!

Getting creative is also a fantastic way to spread kindness. Something that Honey and I love to do, and which you could try, is searching in a nearby park – or beach, if you live near one – for flat, smooth stones to paint. Collect as many as you can, then take them home to decorate with drawings of things you like, or positive words. We write things on our stones, like:

Then you can either keep them for yourself to lift your mood when you need them, or leave them outside for strangers to take as a free gift! It's a lovely, creative way to be kind and spread joy with your clever hands.

TAPPING

When I say the word *tapping*, you probably think about bopping your fingers up and down on something – whether it be a table, door or drum. But did you know that a particular method of tapping your fingers can help you feel happier?

Let's meet our next expert, **Nick Ortner**. He is a tapping therapist and is here to teach us how we can use our fingers to tap lightly on different body parts to make us feel calmer and happier.

Hey, Nick. I'm so interested to learn more about tapping and how it can help us. What exactly is tapping?

Tapping is a technique that you can use to help you feel better in any situation. It involves tapping your fingertips on certain parts of your body while saying particular phrases. So it is a way of bringing your mind and body together to help you feel better, get through a tough situation, sleep better and so much more!

How does it work?

The way it's done is by tapping with your fingertips – however many you'd like, but generally most people use two fingers – on each of the body's nine tapping points while saying certain positive phrases that relate to how you are feeling.

Here are the nine points to tap on your body.

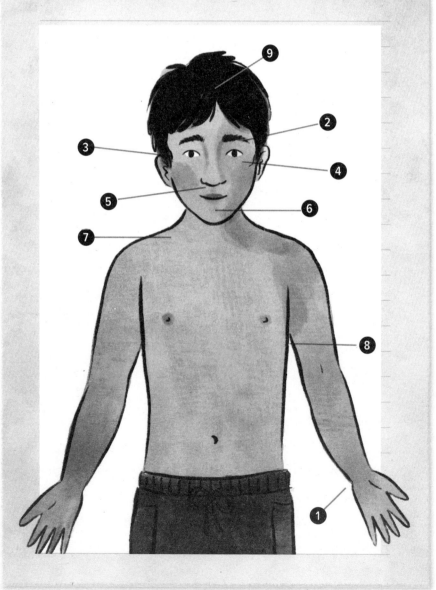

1. Side of the hand – this one is called the karate chop.
2. Eyebrow
3. Side of the eye
4. Under the eye
5. Under the nose
6. Under the mouth
7. Collarbone
8. Under the arm
9. Top of the head

These tapping points are called **meridian points**. Tapping them helps your brain tell your body to calm down. If you're upset and you try tapping, you may feel like you can finally take a deep breath. If you're worried about something, you may start to feel fewer butterflies in your stomach and more focused. The point is, tapping is so easy to do and can help you feel better in any situation you're in!

What is happening in the brain and body when you are using the tapping technique?

When you're feeling stressed, angry, nervous or any other strong emotion, a part of your brain called the

amygdala receives a danger signal. Now, you're not really in danger, but your brain thinks you are. The amygdala is a cluster of cells in the base of your brain that deals with emotion, and when it notices this danger signal it tries to help by releasing hormones like **adrenaline** and **cortisol**. These hormones used to be really important for human survival when we lived in habitats alongside tigers and other fierce predators, but now this stress response isn't needed in the same way! Too much of these hormones can cause you to not think as clearly. Tapping helps to calm the body and brain by decreasing these hormones so you can feel like your 'normal' self again.

How are words used alongside the tapping technique? Why does this help?

Tapping on these points while saying calming affirmations helps send a signal to your brain that everything is OK. The words remind your brain that you are not in danger – there is no tiger! You are just in a situation that is causing you stress, and you can help yourself feel calm in your body and mind. You can follow tapping scripts, or use your own words.

If you are feeling scared, for example, the phrases to repeat might be,

> *I am safe.*

> *I am brave.*

> *I can do hard things.*

What can we use tapping for?

Tapping can be used for anything, particularly to help you in situations that make you feel frustrated, upset, annoyed or disappointed. It can also help when you're having trouble sleeping, or can give you a boost of happiness if needed. It's always worth giving it a try!

The important thing to remember is that it's OK to feel upset, or frustrated or scared. Those are all normal feelings. But when we're feeling scared for so long that it gets in the way of our happiness or stops us reaching our goals, then that's when we need to make a change. Tapping helps us to acknowledge these feelings and stop us feeling stuck in our negative emotions.

TRY THIS!

Tapping is clearly a great way to bring you calmness. In fact, focusing on your sense of touch in lots of other ways can also help calm your nerves and clear your mind. Try it now. Notice what the clothes feel like on your skin. Are they itchy or comforting? Run your hand over the table in front of you – or the floor – and notice what it feels like. Is it smooth or rough? If you're feeling nervous when trying to get to sleep, just notice what the bed beneath you feels like or what the sensation of running your hand over your T-shirt or other hand feels like. It's an easy way to practise being mindful, to focus your mind on your sense of touch and feel calmer. Which – as we know – is very important when trying to tap into your happiness supply!

There are so many cool things you can do with your arms and hands, from communicating to getting creative and tapping. Our hands and sense of touch are amazing and can really help us to feel a lot happier.

TOP TIPS
FOR HAPPY ARMS
AND HANDS:

High-five
yourself every
morning!

Get
creative.

Use your
hands to help
you communicate
and express
yourself.

Practise
tapping.

Use your
sense of touch
to calm nerves
and clear your
mind!

CHAPTER 6

Find your feet

Let's travel down your body to your other limbs: your legs and feet. Our feet are pretty amazing, if you think about it – for example, did you know:

YOU HAVE 26 BONES IN EACH FOOT AND MORE THAN 100 MUSCLES, LIGAMENTS AND TENDONS.

It's time to get to know your feet . . .

Do they stand flat against the ground or is there an arch in your foot?

Are they ticklish?

Can you touch your toes by bending over with your legs straight?

Think of all the incredible things your feet allow you to do.

Today, I laced up my trainers and went on a huge walk through London. I walked over a bridge across the River Thames and then through interesting streets with different-coloured houses. My feet made me very happy today.

But, actually, something that might have made me even happier would have been taking my shoes off! Walking barefoot even has a proper name: **earthing**. If you walk on soil, grass, sand or any other natural surface barefoot, it's said to help with sleep and reducing anxiety. The reason behind this is due to the relationship our bodies have with the earth. When we are in direct contact with it, it has been shown to make us feel a whole lot better.

Grab a parent or carer and ask them if they'll try a short (and safe) barefoot walk with you. Perhaps you could find a nearby patch of grass and make sure you're looking out for any sharp twigs, stones or dog poo. The best place to practise this though – if you're able to – is at the beach. The soft sand against your toes will have you feeling calmer in no time!

In this chapter, I talk about the things that non-disabled people can do with their feet. But not everyone can do these things with ease, and it is really important, if you are a non-disabled person reading this, that you are an ally to people who have a disability. This is all part of making the world a happier place.

Some people are not able to use their legs with ease, or at all, so might use a wheelchair. My friend Sophie Morgan is a brilliant TV presenter and author who can't move her legs or feet, so she uses a wheelchair. She also has the coolest motorbike I've ever seen – she uses her hands to operate the steering and gears and goes on adventurous trips!

What I've learned from talking to Sophie is that the world is often not designed with wheelchair users in mind. For example, many shops and restaurants still do not have ramps or working lifts.

I asked Sophie what I, as a non-disabled person, can be doing to be an ally to wheelchair users and people in the disability community. If you are also not disabled, why not try one of these things too? Here are just a few suggestions for how to make the world a more accessible and happy place for everyone.

1. *Ask adults and teachers about what disability might look like and find out what sorts of questions are OK to ask someone who has a disability.*

2. *Try not to assume that disabled people need your help. Always ask them first.*

3. *If you can't see a ramp, or a disabled loo in your local shop or restaurant, go and ask if there is one, or if they'd be happy to put one in.*

4. *Ask disabled people how they like to talk about their differences. Do they use certain words to describe themselves. Every person will have a different preference.*

5. *Don't touch people's wheelchairs or crutches without asking them first.*

6 If you are playing, think about how you can include disabled friends. Maybe ask them how they like to play or ask your parent or carer for advice.

7 It's OK to use the word 'disabled' – it's not a rude word.

8 Our differences make us who we are and lots of disabled people love their bodies just as they are, so try not to think that they want to be fixed or changed to be non-disabled.

9 It is OK for a disabled person to be upset when they aren't included. Being left out can be tough. Listen to them if they decide to tell you how they feel. It's always important to learn how we can help each other.

10 If someone has an assistance dog ask them before you pet or cuddle it. It is doing a job and can't be distracted, no matter how cute it is.

11 If someone can't see or hear you, ask an adult how best to be friends with them.

I LIKE TO MOVE IT!

Our feet and legs can help us to exercise and move about. You probably learn about exercise at school and have PE lessons, and you might also already know which sport or type of movement you like the best. But how can it help us feel good?

There's no one better to teach us about keeping fit than **Joe Wicks**. Joe has helped so many people get fit with his YouTube workouts. When schools were shut during the Covid-19 pandemic, Joe released 'PE with Joe', his daily online workouts for the whole family. Joe is dedicated to encouraging everyone to give exercise a go to improve physical and mental health, and is going to tell us how moving our bodies is a way of finding joy in each and every day.

Joe Wicks, fitness coach

Hey, Joe. I've done many of your workouts and they've made me feel very happy indeed. When did you discover that you loved exercise?

From the age of about ten I knew I loved exercise, and I was always at an after-school club. Because I had a lot of stress going on at home, after-school clubs and exercise gave me a chance to let out all the frustration I felt. When I was sixteen, I got my first job and joined a gym. I was already on that path of knowing that I loved exercise and I felt safe doing it. I would go home after a workout and I would feel good. I wouldn't be carrying around all that stress and I wouldn't be so confused. I noticed the link between moving and mental health from a young age, and I always understood it could make me feel better and safer.

Why does moving your body make you feel good?

There is so much research that looks at the link between physical activity and our mental health. I'm so passionate about this subject because a lot of the time people only focus on the physical changes they see in their body when it comes to exercise, but there's so much more to it! When you exercise, your brain is releasing chemicals that make you feel good. It could be directly after your workout or a short while afterwards, but you'll notice you start to feel much better, less stressed, a sense of achievement and generally happier. Exercise can really transform how you feel. You will always feel better after a workout and that is what will keep you coming back to do more.

How has exercise helped with your own mental and emotional health?

I did the 'PE with Joe' workouts during the pandemic and, without even realizing, it became my therapy. I thought I was doing it to boost other people's moods but it did the exact same thing for me. Every morning, no matter how I felt, I pushed myself through each daily session and afterwards I felt less stressed, less anxious about the lockdown and my mind felt clearer. I see it like you're physically shaking off negative energy; you're shaking off frustration. When you finish you feel like a different person. It might be a temporary feeling, but you can keep coming back to it with exercise. 'PE with Joe' was such a positive thing for me.

What is your favourite way to move your body?
I get a lot of energy and endorphins from short bursts of exercise. Thirty seconds of doing one move and then thirty seconds rest and then another movement for another quick burst. I love that. I work really hard in these sorts of workouts and the harder I work the better I feel mentally after. I also love walking and cycling. But all movement is good for you. Do the exercise that works for you and makes you feel good.

YOU JUST HAVE TO TAP INTO WHAT YOU LOVE.

If you don't love PE at school or sports, what other types of movement might be fun?

Even if you don't enjoy competitive sport, there are so many other physical activities you might like. Dance, yoga, rock climbing or cycling – the best thing to do is just keep trying new things and see what you like. If it gives you a sense of satisfaction, then you've found your activity. I loved karate as a kid – I started at the age of ten. I loved the challenge of karate and learning new moves and kicks.

PUT ALL YOUR ENERGY INTO THE MOVEMENT YOU LOVE.

There is clearly such a strong link between how much you move and how you FEEL. If we want to access that stash of inner happiness, I know where to start . . .

LET'S GET MOVING!

LISTEN TO YOUR BODY

When you are feeling a little sluggish and don't have much energy, you might want to just chill out in front of the TV or a games console and relax your body. You might even feel like having a nap in the middle of the day. We have to listen to our bodies to understand when we need rest, especially if we have done a lot of exercise that week.

But sometimes we feel tired and there is no opportunity to rest – you might be in the middle of a school day, or on the way to an after-school club and feeling a little sleepy. In these moments you need an energy boost, and here's the cool bit – you can use your feet and legs to help you GAIN energy!

Try it now. If you can, jump up and down on the spot five times. Jump as high as you can, really bending and pushing off from your feet like a springy frog. If you do this a few times, you will hopefully feel like you have more energy inside you. If I am feeling sleepy in the morning before work, I'll often swing my arms round in circles while lifting each leg so my knee moves towards my chest. Move in a way that feels good to you and gives you the energy boost you need.

A form of exercise that can relax your body and boost your mood is something called yoga. Yoga is a very old, beautiful practice – its origins can be traced to northern India over 5,000 years ago! Yoga can help us keep our bodies flexible and strong, and similar to meditation it can also help to calm the brain when it's lost in worries or too many thoughts.

There are many different sorts of yoga, and we're now going to meet our next expert – my friend **Marcia Sharp**, who is a yoga teacher and practises every day. She's going to tell us how yoga can help with happiness!

Marcia Sharp, yoga teacher

Hey, Marcia, can you tell us what exactly yoga is?
Yoga is a practice that helps us move our bodies into different shapes and poses. Sometimes the movement is slow and involves stretches and balances and sometimes it can be slightly quicker. But it is always done gently. It is a wonderful way of looking after your body and mind, benefiting you now and throughout your life. It has been developed by wise men and women over thousands of years and is now practised in every country in the world by people of all ages, shapes and sizes.

Yoga poses and movement help you feel great and become strong and flexible. Yoga can also teach you calming techniques, help you learn about patience and improve your mental health.

With the help of yoga poses, breathing exercises and focus, we can bring harmony to our body and mind, and feel happiness.

Can anyone do yoga?

Yes – if you can breathe, you can do yoga. You probably already do it without realizing, such as when you stretch your arms in the morning, or screw up your face muscles when you yawn.

How does it make you feel?

No matter who you are or how old you are, yoga can help you feel better mentally and physically. Yoga makes all your senses stronger and makes you feel like the best version of you. It helps you to understand yourself and your feelings. Yoga can teach you techniques to manage emotions, like when you might feel a little tired or a bit grumpy, or even to help you feel happy within yourself. To begin with, you may find it funny trying some of the strange yoga shapes, but in time your body and your mind should feel more relaxed and alert!

You can try this exercise to get started:

1. Kneel down resting your forehead on the ground – this is called Child's Pose.

2. Now, imagine there is a glowing light coming from your belly button. You are protecting this light with your body. You need to keep it inside your belly and not let it go.

3. Allow this warming, delightful light to travel through your spine all the way up your back, to your neck and then up to your head.

4. Lift your head a little as you feel the warm light travelling through your body.

5. Raise your head a bit further and gently turn to the left and then to the right (only your head – try to keep the rest of your body still to protect the light in your belly button).

6. Now sit on your heels, place your hands on your belly and feel where the light is coming from. Enjoy the warm sensation in your body.

7. Raise your arms above your head as you breathe in. Imagine that the light is travelling up from your belly button all the way to your hands as you reach up to the sky.

8 As you breathe out, bring your arms back down next to your body.

9 Repeat steps 7 and 8 a few times.

10 Take a moment to enjoy the sensation of a warming light filling up your entire body. Are there any words that come to your mind to describe what you are feeling?

(Inspired by Yoga Games for Children *by Danielle Bersma & Marjoke Visscher.)*

What is happening in our bodies and brains when we take part in yoga?

When we do yoga, we are paying full attention to our body and noticing what we are doing – this means that we are becoming more focused. Doing yoga regularly – like all physical activity – is good for keeping in good physical shape, and managing stress and anxiety. By dedicating some time to looking after your body and mind through yoga, you will be happier and healthier as a result.

What's an exercise we can do to feel calmer?

I'd like you to try an exercise called bubble blowing. This is a really great way of collecting the thoughts that make you feel sad or nervous, and letting them float away – just like a bubble. Pretend that you are surrounded by colourful bubbles. Picture them bobbing and floating around you peacefully. Imagine that you can place any unwanted thought or feeling in one of those bubbles. You could even say to yourself, 'this thought is making me worried. I'm going to put it in a bubble and watch it float off into the distance.' Start to breathe in slowly, then imagine the bubble as it floats away, becoming smaller and smaller, until it pops.

Our thoughts and feelings are just like bubbles: they come up, and they drift away.

Sometimes they POP.

(Inspired by Mindfulness Activities for Kids – https://www.healthline.com/health/mind-body/mindfulness-activities.)

Why is breathing in a certain way important in yoga?

Yoga teaches us ways of breathing that slow your heart rate and lower your blood pressure, which can make you feel calmer. Yogic breathing can also improve your concentration and even how good you are at sports!

What are some good breathing exercises to practise?

1. WATCH YOUR BREATH

Find something small and light to hold in the palm of your hand. It can be a feather, a small piece of tissue or a cottonwool ball. Place your hand under your nose. Start to breathe in and out through your nose and watch your object. Does it move away from you as you breathe out? Is it closer as you breathe in? Now try to breathe through your mouth and watch your object. Can you tell whether you are breathing in or out from the way it moves around? Do you notice any difference if you breathe with your mouth, instead of your nose, or if you take smaller or bigger breaths?

Based on *Yoga Games for Children* by Danielle Bersma & Marjoke Visscher.

2. DRAGON BREATHING

You can try this fun exercise standing up, kneeling or sitting down. Take a deep breath in to fill your chest and your belly. Take your time counting to 3 and then breathe out very slowly from your mouth. As you breathe out imagine that you are a dragon breathing out fire. Make a long, slow 'hah' sound as you exhale. How are you feeling? More relaxed, I hope!

Based on *Mindfulness Activities for Kids.*
https://www.healthline.com/health/mind-body/mindfulness-activities

What if I'm not very flexible? Can I still do yoga?

We are all different both physically and mentally – the beauty of yoga is that it is for everyone. It doesn't really matter if you aren't flexible at the beginning – you can do yoga to gain flexibility and strength. Stick with it and learn to appreciate your body and what it is capable of. You can develop at your own pace with no judgement from others.

REMEMBER: YOU HAVE AN ENTIRE LIFETIME TO KEEP IMPROVING AND PRACTISING YOGA CAN HELP YOU REACH YOUR HAPPY PLACE.

It's fascinating to learn about how moving your body in different ways can help you feel energized but also calm. You can jump in the air and move your limbs to gain energy but you can also move slowly to calm your body and mind. The most important thing to do is listen to your body – does it need an energy boost? Do you need to relax? Do you need to spend five minutes moving around in order to lift your mood? Take a second to listen to what your body is asking for, then try out different movements and see what helps!

RUNNING AWAY

By now we know that our legs and feet can help us to move in ways that make us feel good. But what about those times when we feel like running from a situation because we are worried or scared? Sometimes we are not sure whether to run away from a nerve-wracking situation, or to stay and try and face the fear. But often the thing we're scared of is not quite as scary when we face up to it, and sometimes being involved in these situations can be really helpful.

Recently, Rex was very nervous about going on a school trip as he didn't feel comfortable staying overnight. He wanted to run from the situation. When we feel like running from things we are scared of, we are in what is called fight-or-flight mode. Humans have this inbuilt response to scary situations due to the dangers that threatened survival for our ancient ancestors. Fight-or-flight mode kicks in when we face a situation that makes us feel we are in danger. It keeps us super alert and on our toes. Our breath quickens and our heart beats faster so that we are ready to run from danger. Our ancestors really needed this so that they could run away from predatory animals without a second thought. We might not be running away from giant bears or tigers in the wild any more but our bodies react as if we are. It's all very normal and most people experience this at some point.

But I am glad to say Rex did not run away. He faced up to his fear of staying overnight on the school trip and he had a wonderful time. He now feels so much more confident and far less scared about his next school trip.

When we want to run away from situations, it can be helpful to talk it through with someone. Having fears is a normal part of life for everyone, but sometimes all it takes is a conversation with someone who cares to show you that something might not be so scary after all. And once you do it, you'll also feel more confident about doing it again in the future!

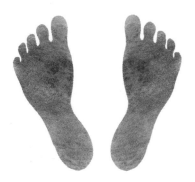

I HOPE YOU AREN'T TICKLISH ...

Did you know your feet are connected to many other parts of your body? Have you ever heard of reflexology? It's a type of foot massage that allows the practitioner to feel whether you have tension in other body areas. The reflexologist (person who performs reflexology) touches certain areas of your feet and can then tell what is going on around your body. For example, a part of the big toe is related to the head. If there is tension in the big toe, then you might be suffering from headaches. Or the practitioner might feel a bit of tension in the arch of your foot, which relates to the stomach and might mean you are suffering from stomach aches. Although reflexologists do not diagnose illnesses, they can certainly help to soothe and relax you and your body by massaging away any tension.

If you aren't too ticklish, why not get someone in your family to massage your feet at bedtime? It doesn't need to be for long, but it can be very relaxing. Make sure your feet aren't too cheesy – it's always a good idea to wash your feet in the bath or shower first – then get someone to either rub your feet or push down on certain points.

Or you could try it yourself! Press down gently on different areas of your foot to see how it feels in both your feet and the rest of your body.

Ahhhhhh, bliss!

ENERGY

Energy is coursing through our bodies all the time. It's not something we can see or scientifically pin down, but many cultures look at how this energy is flowing to improve wellness. In traditional Chinese medicine there is a lot of focus on the energy running through our body, which is called qi or chi (pronounced 'chee'). People who practise this type of medicine are able to feel if there are blockages where your energy is not flowing as it should.

There is a treatment called acupuncture, which involves the practitioner placing tiny, thin needles into the surface of your skin, which they often then twist to aid the flow of energy. It might sound painful and scary but it really doesn't hurt much at all. You feel a little prick as the needles touch your skin but it's not massively uncomfortable, and it can help if you feel that your body or emotions are a little out of balance.

Acupressure is when you push down gently on certain body parts to help release tension (a little bit like reflexology does with your feet). If you are feeling nervous or stressed, try massaging your own jaw, as sometimes we hold a lot of tension in our jaws. Put your fingers just below your ears and move them downwards towards your chin, lightly rubbing in circular motions to help loosen up the muscles. This can really improve relaxation and energy flow.

You can also squeeze the skin in-between your thumb and index finger to help you relax. Stretch one hand out and gently squeeze the webbed area using the thumb and index finger on the other hand. It feels squishy and a little strange to touch. You can do this to help calm your nerves. Like we've tried with all the other senses, focus on touch in this moment and allow your mind to calm down and release some worries.

Although we don't have any vital organs in our legs and feet, and even though they are the furthest body parts from our brain, they really are quite amazing. And very useful in helping us feel happier. They enable us to do so much and are cleverly connected to the rest of our body. I have learned so much about feet while writing this chapter that I'm going to try to spend a lot more time with my toes out rather than hidden away in shoes.

When you can, whip off those socks and admire what beauties your feet are!

We have now travelled around the entire human body! Let's step back for a minute and just admire how amazing it really is.

TOP TIPS
FOR HAPPY FEET:

If you are non-disabled, be an ally to your disabled peers and help make the world a more accessible and happy place.

Try earthing to feel happy and charged by Planet Earth.

Find the sport or activity that makes you feel GREAT.

Experiment with massaging your feet to feel calm before bed.

Breathe like a dragon!

Remember things are a lot less scary once you've tried them.

Stretch your muscles out and try practising yoga.

Use your sense of touch to calm nerves and clear your mind!

THE END OF OUR
ADVENTURE

Because I'm telling you now – your body is extraordinary.

Each one of us on Planet Earth is unique. We are different heights, different sizes and shapes, have different skin tones, different-shaped eyes, noses and mouths – we even have completely unique fingerprints that you won't share with anyone else on the planet. See how special you are?

Sometimes we feel embarrassed about our bodies, and we think there is something not quite right about them. But all these differences are what makes us interesting as humans! And it's important to remember this, as no one should EVER let their worries about the way their body looks get in the way of their happiness. Don't feel weird about looking at it in the mirror and admiring all the wonderful things it can do. If you don't tell yourself how brilliant your body is, then who will?

Don't feel odd practising your breathing, tapping, or mindfulness – it will only bring you closer to finding joy in each and every day. Now that you have these incredible techniques from the talented experts we met on our journey, USE THEM! Sometimes life is challenging and we find ourselves feeling like happiness is very far away. That's OK. Feeling a whole range of emotions is completely normal and a part of life. If we aim to feel only happiness all the time we might be missing out on some other cool experiences. Some of the best songs out there have been written when the musician has felt very sad, and some artists have painted the most beautiful paintings because they felt angry or passionate about something. Some inventors have created incredible machinery or technology because they felt annoyed that something was missing in their life. Each emotion has worth and can teach us something interesting about ourselves and life.

Next time you feel angry, see if there's a positive place that it leads you to. Maybe it will motivate you to run faster or find solutions to a frustrating problem. There are positive ways to look at all our emotions. It might feel much nicer to be happy, but there is so much to discover in all the feelings we go through.

But, as we all know, happiness is the best. And if you ever feel like you are a little stuck in one emotion and need some help tapping into your happiness supply, then you might want to try using something you've learned from this book! If you are stuck in worry or anger, you might want to try one of the calming techniques like Nick's tapping or Rebecca's breathing. If you find yourself stuck in sadness, you might want to take Joe's advice on how good exercise can make you feel. Happiness is a great feeling that we all want to experience more. Sometimes we know when it's going to show up and on other occasions it's a total surprise. The other morning we were late for school and rushing to get out of the car. We were all a little moody. Rex hates being rushed, and Honey dislikes being late as she doesn't want to get into trouble. I was stressed out and not feeling that happy at all, but as we dashed up the road to the school, I slipped on some ice and nearly fell over. We all laughed ... A LOT! We looked down and one part of the pavement was covered in slippery ice. We pretended we were ice skating and wobbled and wibbled our way across the pavement to the school gates. That's the cool thing about happiness – we can never be sure when it's going to show up.

Thank you so much for coming on this adventure with me. It's been so much fun to explore the body from head to toe with you (even those of you with cheesy feet). Remember: your body is amazing and can help you experience so much happiness in life if you look after it. So wherever your happiness is stored, hopefully this book has shown you how to find the tools to access it.

You and your body really are brilliant, from head to toe!

Acknowledgements

Writing this book has been so interesting. I've learned so much from the experts and people I interviewed and hope you did too. I want to start by thanking the contributors for their time and wisdom. What a beautiful bunch! Kimberley Wilson, Tom Daley, Adam Martin, Betsy Griffin, Jono Lancaster, Tom Fletcher, Rebecca Dennis, Rhiannon Lambert, Nick Ortner, Joe Wicks and Marcia Sharp, I'm forever grateful.

Thank you Phoebe Jascourt and Pippa Shaw at Penguin Random House for supporting me in the writing of this book. It was a gift to have your guidance and diligence throughout the process and wonderful to hear that you were equally excited by what our experts had to offer.

Thank you to Jan Bielecki and Sophie Stericker for their wonderful design work, and to Stef Murphy who brought this book to life with her brilliant illustrations. These wonderful drawings helped create a proper journey through the human body and also captured our guests perfectly.

Thank you to Amanda Harris at YMU Group for being the most incredible literary agent around. Not only incredibly knowledgeable about all things book, but also a mother to three amazing kids. Having Amanda's full-bodied understanding of this subject matter has been invaluable. I'm so excited to see where we can take Happy Place Books next.

Thank you to Mary Bekhait, Holly Bott and Sarah White at YMU Group for the most sensational triangle of support for all of my projects. I am unbelievably lucky to have you three women in my life.

There are some very special people I want to thank now and they are Rex, Honey, Arthur and Lola. Although my stepchildren Arthur and Lola are now twenty and seventeen years old, I have been lucky enough to watch them grow up from the ages of nine and five. It has been a privilege and has taught me so much in my parenting journey. Rex and Honey thank you for teaching me cool stuff every day. Whether it's things you've learned at school or huge questions you ask me that leave me pondering for days, I'm beyond grateful for your expansive mindsets and deep curiosity. So much of that curiosity led me to write this book and try and work out the answers to some of the questions you've asked. I love you little monkeys so much.

Thank you to my husband Jesse who is always a great support when I'm writing. He makes a mean coffee when I'm losing my way and also has calming advice on hand.

Now it's time for me to thank YOU. Thank you so much for picking up this book and giving it a go. I really hope you enjoyed our journey through the body and that it has started some interesting conversations between you and your family and friends. You and your body are brilliant!

I want to finish off by thanking my body. Without it I wouldn't have been able to type the words with my fingers, think up the ideas with my brain, see the information in front of me, or hear the feedback from my team. Thank you, body. Don't forget to thank yours too!

Here's a quick reminder of the brilliant and clever people who I interviewed for this book. Make sure you check out their books, podcasts, social media pages and websites if you'd like to learn more about them!

Kimberley Wilson, psychologist and nutritionist

Tom Daley, Olympic diver

Adam Martin, meditation teacher

Betsy Griffin, YouTube star

Jono Lancaster, speaker and charity founder

Tom Fletcher, songwriter and author

Rhiannon Lambert, registered nutritionist and author

Rebecca Dennis, breath coach

Joe Wicks, fitness coach

Nick Ortner, tapping coach

Marcia Sharp, yoga teacher

Resources

If you'd like to know a bit more about the things you've read in this book, or read some of the other books and websites that I've mentioned, then here are some resources you might find helpful:

A Different Sort of Normal by Abigail Balfe

This is a wonderful and true story of one girl's journey growing up autistic – and the challenges she faced in the 'normal' world. It's a great book for readers aged nine and over to help you understand autism, and for young people who have ever felt like they don't fit in.

Health For Kids

This NHS website has lots of fun games, articles and activities to help you learn about your feelings and looking after yourself.

healthforkids.co.uk/feelings

KidsHealth

This fact-packed website can help you understand everything about your body – from how it works, to staying healthy and growing up. If you click 'for kids', it will take you to the part of the website with information written for children.

kidshealth.org

Change4Life

This fantastic website tells you all about how to eat healthily and exercise in order to keep your to keep your body and mind feeling great.

change4life.co.uk

Childline

Childline is a free and private service for anyone under the age of nineteen. You can get information about feelings, bullying and more on their website. They have a free 24-hour helpline you can call to talk to a counsellor about anything that's worrying you.

childline.org.uk

0800 1111

YoungMinds

YoungMinds is an organisation that provides mental health support to children and teenagers. Young people can find lots of information on their website. They provide a 24/7 crisis text service for young people – if you need urgent help, you can text YM to 85258.

youngminds.org.uk

Autism Education Trust

If you want to learn more about autism, or how to support autistic people, this website has tons of useful information.

autismeducationtrust.org.uk

Yoga Games For Children by Danielle Bersma and Marjoke Visscher

This is a fun introduction to yoga for children that will help readers develop strength, flexibility, calmness and much more. It's perfect for readers aged six and over.

Mindfulness Activities for Kids

This website has a huge list of mindfulness activities for people of all ages. They are designed to relieve stress and help you be more present in the moment.

healthline.com/health/mind-body/mindfulness-activities